STRATEGIC
MARKET
PLANNING

STRATEGIC MARKET PLANNING

Robert J. Hamper • L. Sue Baugh

Printed on recyclable paper

NTC Business Books
NTC/Contemporary Publishing Company

Library of Congress Cataloging-in-Publication Data
is available from the United States Library of Congress.

This edition published 1998 by NTC Business Books
An imprint of NTC/Contemporary Publishing Company
4255 West Touhy Avenue, Lincolnwood (Chicago), Illinois 60646-1975 U.S.A.
Copyright © 1990 by NTC/Contemporary Publishing Company
Printed in the United States of America
International Standard Book Number: 0-8442-3215-7; 0-8442-3216-5 (pbk.)
20   19   18   17   16   15   14   13   12   11   10   9   8   7   6

To Bert and Sadie,
whose friendship was always there

To all marketing managers and their staffs,
for whom this book was written

Contents

Foreword

Occasionally, my eight-year-old son comes home with a four-letter word he uses but doesn't understand. In business, it's funny how the same thing can happen. People use a four-letter word like *plan* all the time without really understanding its meaning.

With my son, a good talking to and maybe a half hour in the corner will solve the problem. In the second case, I suggest a good talking to as well, but not until you've read Hamper and Baugh's *Strategic Market Planning*.

These two authors have collaborated on a solid working document detailing the who, what, why, and how of creating a strategic plan. The book concentrates on the planning *process*, which is often the most critical aspect of doing realistic and successful planning.

In my capacity as vice president of marketing and sales at Quaker Oats, I come in contact with a wide variety of companies. Despite all the writing and teaching that has been done on the need for planning, I am always amazed at how misunderstood and misapplied this concept is in the business world.

Often what passes for a "plan" is merely a compilation of wishful thinking and grandiose financial projections designed to secure needed funds. It has little to do with the strategic aspects of successfully operating a business. And the fault is not limited to smaller companies. Even large corporations, which are touted for their planning prowess, often fail to plan at the strategic level.

Strategic Market Planning can help correct this oversight. There is something in this book to benefit everyone—the first-time planner, the business student, the entrepreneur, or the seasoned pro.

The entrepreneur needs to read this book and become familiar with the strategic planning process for two reasons: as a prerequisite for financial backing and, more importantly, as a way of achieving long-term success.

The seasoned pro who has been "planning" for years will find reassurance for what he or she has been doing right and encouragement for how much can be done better.

These two authors have gone straight to the heart of the planning process. In my opinion, they provide the best insights into making the four-letter word *plan* useful, understandable, and comfortable for everyone involved.

Paul V. Baron
Vice President, Marketing & Sales
Quaker Oats Company

Preface

Strategic Market Planning offers a step-by-step explanation of how to build a dynamic, future-oriented marketing plan for your company. In this book we provide the following:

- An overview of the planning process and the role of market planning.
- Qualitative tools to help you determine company mission and goals.
- Quantitative tools to pinpoint your firm's strengths, weaknesses, and resources; to take stock of the competitive situation and business environment; and to assess your risks and opportunities.
- Questionnaires and forms to generate the data you need to create a three- to five-year marketing plan for your firm.
- A running sample case to illustrate the principles in each chapter and to provide examples of completed questionnaires, forms, and matrices.

To help you develop your marketing plan, we cover the following topics:

Part One: The Planning Process—an overview of the entire planning process within a firm.

Part Two: Four-Step Environmental Assessment—situation analysis, product positioning, portfolio analysis, problem and opportunity analysis. This section starts with a close look at the external and internal environment of your firm and its market situation, determines strengths and weaknesses, and begins to formulate opportunities on which you can focus.

Part Three: Developing the Plan—In this section we help you to set marketing objectives for your firm, select the market segments your firm should target and the products it should develop, and choose marketing strategies that will help your firm succeed.

Part Four: Implementation and Control—Many good plans fail because they are poorly implemented and communicated to the people responsible for carrying them out. This section shows you common pitfalls to avoid and provides guidelines to make sure your plan gets off to a sound start. We also cover setting up sound control and monitoring systems to evaluate the effectiveness of your plan as it is implemented.

Appendix: Forms and instructions are provided at the end of the book to help you gather data to develop your strategic marketing plan.

How to Use This Book

We have designed *Strategic Market Planning* as a practical guide through the planning process. It is not intended to give you in-depth marketing theory nor to discuss strategic alternatives and tactics under a wide variety of conditions.

The emphasis is on developing a proactive marketing plan that will give your firm a blueprint for future growth. To get the greatest benefit from *Strategic Market Planning,* we recommend that you follow these steps:

1. Read through the chapter material before filling out any questionnaires, checklists, or diagrams. Get familiar with the topics discussed and make sure you understand what information you are being asked to gather.

2. Realize that finding out what you *don't* know is as valuable as the information you *do* know. Gaps in data can often reveal a company's problems and weaknesses. Use the questionnaires, checklists, and diagrams to discover what you need to learn about your company operations, the competition, and the marketplace.

Make sure managers and staff have a chance to review the completed forms and make comments. The more broad-based your data are within the company, the more accurate and sound they are likely to be.

3. Work through the book in sequence. A common mistake in developing plans is to skip steps. The data you develop for each step in the marketing plan will serve as a starting point for the next step.

We wish you the best as you develop your strategic marketing plan!

Acknowledgments

We gratefully acknowledge the assistance of the following people in the development of this book:

Don E. Schultz, Ph.D., Professor of Advertising at the Medill School of Journalism, Advertising Division, Northwestern University, Evanston, Illinois.

Nona Mary Allard, O.P., Associate Professor of Mathematics, Rosary College, River Forest, Illinois.

Patricia A. McDonough, M.B.A., Corporate Management Consultant, Chicago, Illinois.

These individuals gave generously of their time and advice throughout the writing process. Their many suggestions and comments proved invaluable as we developed the book.

Special acknowledgments to Norm Zuefle for his support and encouragement during the writing of this book and to Dorothy Creed for her careful copyediting of the manuscript.

Robert J. Hamper
River Forest, Illinois

L. Sue Baugh
Evanston, Illinois

PART ONE

Planning Process

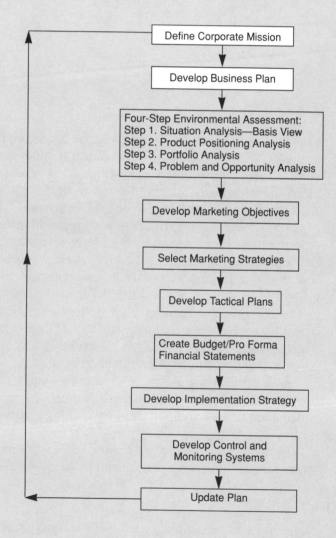

CHAPTER ONE

Getting Started

Introduction

The pace of social and economic change is accelerating, and with it, the risks of doing business. Competition is stiffer. Industries are becoming more concentrated. In a world of look-alike products and services, your company must find a way to stand out. You must hit the right target market with exactly the right product.

To succeed, your firm needs accurate marketing information to determine consumer needs, to identify your markets, and to offer the best products and services. These efforts must be coordinated by a sound marketing plan that can help your company to achieve its twin goals of increased profit and a healthy market share.

Many company managers find themselves at a loss when it comes to putting together a marketing plan. Part of the problem is that some managers do not fully understand the function of marketing and the process of active, future-oriented market planning.

As a result, they are merely *reactive*—trying to keep up with changing conditions. Instead, they must become *proactive*—anticipating those conditions and developing a plan of action for the future.

In this chapter, we provide an overview of marketing and describe the planning process followed by many successful companies.

What Is Marketing?

Marketing can be defined broadly as the function within a company that seeks to generate a profit by organizing the firm's resources and activities to determine and satisfy the needs and desires of consumers.

In the past, marketing was regarded as synonymous with selling and advertising. Today, marketing is considered a management function. Marketing executives and other company managers decide how company resources should be used to achieve customer satisfaction and specific profit goals. Advertising and promotion usually support marketing efforts.

Notice that the emphasis is on *profits* rather than merely on *sales*. Companies are not seeking an increase in volume per se; they are more interested in the return on each item sold. As a result, they must focus their efforts on finding the consumers most likely to buy their product. Marketing must determine the following:

- Who the customers are and what they need and want.
- When they want it.
- Where they want it.
- How they want to buy it; what price they are willing to pay.

These points make up the 4 P's of marketing, called the *marketing mix:* Product, Promotion, Place (distribution), and Price. The 4 P's are what the marketing manager considers controllable variables; that is, they can be adjusted and changed in determining strategies for the firm and for the products and services the firm wishes to market.

The Marketing Concept

The marketing concept reflects the current shift from production-oriented policies to a consumer- or marketing-oriented approach. Briefly defined, the *marketing concept* is a management philosophy which states that the key task of the company is to discover what various target markets want and need, and to deliver the desired products and services more effectively and efficiently to those markets than does the competition.

In the past, firms organized their resources to make and design products virtually in a vacuum. Advertising and promotion were then responsible for "pushing" products or services through the market by creating consumer demand for them. We were sold novelties, electrical gadgets, and hundreds of other items we suddenly couldn't do without. Through the boom years of the 1950s and 1960s, companies used the push strategy to capture market share.

In the 1970s and 1980s, however, the economy underwent a series of shocks. Two severe recessions, an energy crisis, and foreign competition brought an end to the fantasy of an ever-expanding product market. Today, more and more industries are dominated by fewer and fewer large companies, while the remaining firms scramble to find and fill market segments and niches. Competition for the consumer dollar has made it vital to discover what particular customer groups want and to meet their needs.

As a result, the corporate marketing strategy has changed from "pushing" products through the market to "pulling" them through. In a pull strategy, companies pinpoint consumer demand (for electronic games, for example), then manufacture the product, and let consumer demand pull it through the market. Promotion and advertising are aimed at consumers who have already been identified by market research. The goal is to increase consumer awareness of the product and persuade buyers that it will fulfill their needs and wants. While certainly not foolproof, the pull strategy has proved successful for many companies.

The principle is clear. A firm using the marketing concept has the potential to grow at a much faster rate than a production-orientated firm, since its basic input for planning and product development is from the consumer.

The marketing concept requires that a company adopt an integrated approach to planning and execution that includes the entire management structure from senior executives to field salespeople. The concept marshalls total personnel and material resources toward the dual end of satisfying consumer needs and achieving the company's profit goals. With this approach in place, firms establish a central company mission that serves as a focal point for all management, produce correct products for each market, and look forward to achieving their sales and profit goals. The key to this process is good planning.

Company Planning Process

The company planning process creates a hierarchy of plans beginning with the business plan, moving to the marketing plan, and finishing with individual product plans. Figure 1.1 summarizes the interactive nature of this process and the scope of the three plans.

Once a sound planning cycle is established in a company, the firm can revise, update, and alter its plans on a regular basis.

Key Factors in a Successful Planning Process

If a company is just beginning to realize the need for strategic planning, several key factors are essential in creating a successful planning process.

First, management must clearly see the need for change. Perhaps the company is losing key customers or experiencing a steady erosion of market share. Sales may be flat or earnings declining. Whatever the

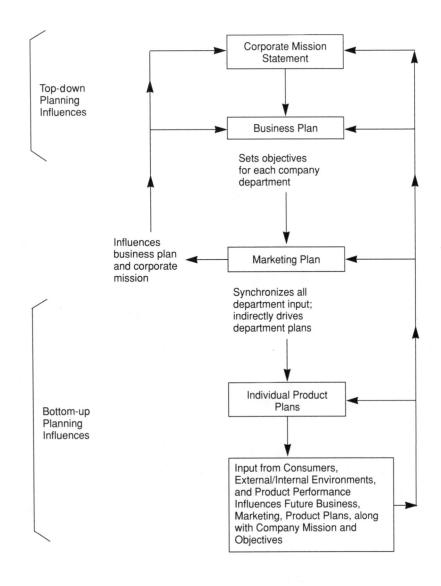

Figure 1.1 Company Planning Process and Hierarchy of Plans

indicator, management must feel that it is serious enough to take decisive action.

Second, someone or some group must "champion" the idea that the company needs to change through strategic market planning. The marketing manager, financial manager, or other advocate for change in the company must persuade top management that the firm needs to change and explain the benefits and advantages of accomplishing it through market planning. Without a champion, it is doubtful that management will agree to initiate and carry through a planning process.

Third, the planning process must have high credibility with all levels of management and all users. This can best be done by involving middle and line managers and other users from the beginning, asking for their input, listening to their concerns and suggestions. The planning influences from top and bottom, as shown in Figure 1.1, must be melded to help the company set goals that all departments can meet.

Fourth, the finished plans must be realistic and reflect the actual resources and capabilities of each department and of the company as a whole. Also, planners should keep managers and users abreast of changes and additions to the plans as they are made.

Fifth, managers and other users should be trained in any procedures essential to the planning process. These procedures include methods of data gathering, analysis, and interpretation; development of budgets or forecasts; and accomplishment of other tasks vital to a successful planning process. Without some systematic method of gathering and assembling data, strategic planning is far more difficult. Company personnel should understand what information is needed and in what form.

Finally, written plans must be concise and well organized. Managers and users should be able to understand quickly the purpose of the plan, their assigned responsibilities, and the end results desired. The more concise and clear the plan, the more likely it will be carried out successfully.

It is important to understand that the planning cycle in a successful firm is not a strict, linear process. Instead, as shown in Figure 1.1, it is highly interactive among all levels. It can be seen as a spiral, with constant adjustments made to the company mission, objectives, and plans in response to changing internal and external factors. The driving force of the cycle is company goals and consumer response.

Defining Company Mission

Once the need for planning has been established, the company must determine its mission. A company's *mission statement* defines what kind of firm its owners or managers want it to be, what business it is in, and what its broad-ranged goals are. As shown in Figure 1.1, the mission statement must be in place before you can begin to design any written plans.

Defining the mission takes place at the highest level of the planning hierarchy. Companies from small, entrepreneurial enterprises to corporate giants spend considerable time developing and refining this statement. For example, a major auto company's mission statement reads as follows:

The fundamental purpose of our corporation is to provide products and services of such quality that our customers will receive superior value, our employees and business partners will share in our success, and our stockholders will receive a sustained, superior return on their investment.

The importance of this step cannot be overstated. If the mission is defined too narrowly, it may hamper the firm's growth. AT&T, for example, can no longer say that its mission is to be number one in the telephone business. Since their court-ordered breakup, they are now competing with many other firms. As a result, industry observers have claimed that their new mission is to be a leader in the telecommunications/systems business. This mission enables them to build on their core business, long distance, and branch outward into communications/information systems for further growth.

The mission statement must be updated periodically to make sure that it still defines the best course for the company. The more rapid the pace of change in a market or industry, the more often the mission statement will need to be reexamined. All top level managers must clearly understand the mission statement and accept its definition. No amount of planning can help your firm prosper unless you know what business you are in and what you want to accomplish.

Look over the mission statement for DataStar at the end of the Sample Case. We suggest that you try your hand at writing your own company's mission statement on Form 1: Mission Statement found in the Appendix. Even if the statement is only in rough form, it will help you to clarify your thinking about your business and your overall goals. That knowledge will act as a backdrop for the work you will be doing throughout the rest of this book.

Objectives and Strategies

Once the company mission is defined, management must then translate that mission into a set of *objectives*, or goals, that become the basis for the business plan. Suppose, for example, that AT&T's stated mission is to be a leader in the telecommunications/systems business. It must translate that statement into objectives such as these:

1. Expand into new consumer markets.
2. Develop new business communications services.
3. Explore possible overseas telecommunications linkups with foreign companies.

Notice that these objectives are more specific than the mission statement. They represent overall goals that the company wishes to achieve, goals that will shape the direction and operations of the entire business. These goals must be

1. Reasonable—based on the realities of the market and capabilities of the firm.
2. Obtainable—within reach of the company given its resources and personnel.
3. Measurable—yielding results that can be measured against projections or some accepted company yardstick.

However, objectives are still general. They state *what* the company wants to accomplish, but not *how* it will do so. Strategies spell out how to meet goals.

Strategies are more specific than objectives and determine the overall design or program for achieving goals, whether for a company or a division, for a product or product line. Strategies are usually linked to definite periods of time—a year, three years, five years. In our AT&T example, for instance, the strategies for the first objective might include these:

1. Segment the consumer market into categories of target markets.
2. Identify specific consumer wants and needs.
3. Develop products within two years to meet those needs.
4. Achieve a certain percentage on shareholder equity.

As you can see, the basic strategy is to target specific consumer groups rather than to blanket the entire market with products and then determine which ones succeed.

In the planning process, strategies at a higher level become objectives for the level immediately below. For instance, business plan strategies become objectives for the departmental level and ultimately for the marketing plan. In turn, departmental level strategies become objectives for individual product plans. As objectives and strategies move down the corporate ladder, they become more detailed and specific.

Company Planning Hierarchy

The business, marketing, and product plans make up the planning hierarchy of the firm. We discuss each of these plans briefly, since many managers confuse their purpose and function.

The Business Plan

The *business plan* is a written document that spells out in detail the current status of a company's business and, more importantly, where the company is headed. It forces management to identify opportunities and threats, to recognize the firm's strengths and weaknesses, to reconcile conflicting views, and to arrive at a set of agreed-upon goals and strategies for the company in a systematic and realistic way.

The business plan is prepared by top management and covers all aspects of the business: overall goals, strategies, market forecasts, pro forma financial statements, products, and any other aspects. It is the master plan from which all other plans arise. This document is not cast in stone, however. In a proactive firm, the plan will be influenced by input from the marketing and product plans as they are developed and implemented. Thus, the firm can adjust continually to information from the marketplace and maintain a dynamic, interactive planning process from year to year.

The Marketing Plan

After the business plan is developed, the marketing plan must be defined and written. Market planning is a specialized function in the overall business planning. The importance of marketing is that it serves as the major link between the business firm and its environment.

The *marketing plan* can be thought of as the company's blueprint for future growth and success. In developing it, you survey the economic and competitive environment, isolate marketing opportunities, and state a course of action to take advantage of those opportunities. The plans of other departments support the marketing plan. The marketing plan, in turn, influences and modifies other departmental plans, e.g., cost of programs, number of units for production department, number of employees for personnel department. All of these plans directly and indirectly influence the overall business plan of the company.

As the company's objectives and strategies are translated into marketing objectives, strategic market planning is developed. *Strategic planning* is a commitment on the part of management to look into future market conditions and determine among other things the products and services that should be offered, dropped, maintained, or redirected to new segments. Strategic planning can be short term (one to three years) or long term (three to seven years). Tactical plans to achieve marketing strategies are usually set for less than one year.

As the company's blueprint, the marketing plan defines goals, procedures, and methods that will determine the company's future. It identifies the most promising business opportunities for the firm. It outlines how to penetrate, capture, and maintain desired positions in identified markets. The effectiveness of the marketing plan depends on two factors:

1. Level of commitment by all those who must work for its success.
2. Degree that it keeps abreast of changes in the market environment. Planning is always a continuous process.

The marketing plan also serves as a communications tool that integrates and coordinates elements of the marketing mix: product, place, price, and promotion. It specifies by product, region, and market who will do what, where, when, and how to achieve the company's goals as stated in the business plan.

A successful marketing plan must be

- Simple—easy to understand and communicate.
- Clear—precise and detailed.
- Practical—realistic in its application and goal attainment.
- Flexible—adjusting to changing conditions.
- Complete—covering all significant marketing factors.
- Workable—identifying responsibilities.

The Product Plan

Individual *product plans* are the final and lowest level of planning related to marketing. The product plan is used to analyze product performance and establish product objectives, strategies, and tactics aimed at meeting the overall marketing plan strategies. Product plans also provide ways to determine profit and derivation of net profit.

If a firm has a limited product line, the product plan is often incorporated into the marketing plan. Firms with many lines of business, products, or markets will develop individual product plans as separate documents, each supporting the marketing plan. The final goal is the coordination of all product plans to fulfill the objectives and strategies of the marketing plan.

Separating Marketing Plans from Product Plans

At first glance, it may seem like duplication to prepare a marketing plan and separate product plans. This may be true in smaller companies with limited product lines; but in larger firms with many products and a variety of markets, each product plan can be extremely complex. A single marketing plan is needed to control and guide all these plans toward achieving company objectives.

There are many good reasons for separating the marketing plan from individual product plans. A separate product plan helps the product group clarify its action programs and encourages group involvement and commitment to the plan. It also integrates product management activity in the total planning effort. However, only those concerns and tasks that relate directly to a product should be included in the plan.

Market Planning Cycle

The market planning cycle takes place within the larger company-wide planning cycle. In a marketing-oriented firm, consumer needs and wants drive the market planning cycle. As shown in Figure 1.2, the cycle begins by determining what goods and services consumers want. All other steps follow from this information. The feedback loop that drives the cycle is consumer reaction to the products. Are consumers satisfied? If not, what product changes need to be made? How can the product or service be improved?

Proactive versus Reactive Marketing Plans

The marketing plan should be a proactive document that clearly states the firm's growth objectives. By *proactive*, we mean the company takes the initiative by determining to be a leader, not a follower, in a high-potential market.

A *reactive* approach usually indicates that planning is taking place at the tactical level, too far down the planning hierarchy to affect company-wide policy. The firm also is adopting a defensive position, reacting to changes rather than determining its own future.

When planning occurs primarily at the tactical level, the company possesses a myopic view of the market. Planning may be based on a single product or product line. The results are potentially disastrous: growth slows, profits decrease, market share declines. For example, suppose your competitor is constantly gathering market research information to determine consumers' current and future wants and needs. The competitor develops new products and offers them in the market. Your firm must now respond by spending considerable money to retool production lines, create promotional campaigns, and introduce new products in a short time.

The result: lower profit margins and smaller market share because you were late in entering the market. You were reacting to your competitor's actions and to the market rather than having a more aggressive, proactive plan. This is not to imply that you have to be first in

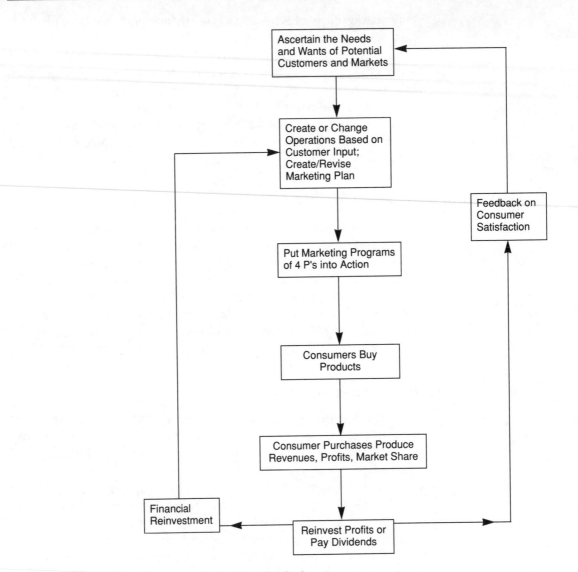

Figure 1.2 Market Planning Cycle

every market. But your company must stay abreast of market changes. This approach minimizes reactive planning by creating a proactive marketing plan geared to the future. Too much reactive planning has been the death of many firms.

What about the company who must be a market follower, creating its own niche? The principle is the same. To be a successful niche company, you must have a future-oriented marketing plan.

If you know opportunities exist but are seeing the competition seize them, you need to take stock of your planning process. It could be that you are reacting to limited, day-to-day changes and information instead of planning for the future.

Benefits of a Marketing Plan

A good marketing plan explains what is to be done, where it is to be done, and who is to do each function. It eliminates confusion and makes work easier and more efficient. It increases motivation and productivity by stressing a team approach to achieving goals.

Formulating an organized and well-conceived marketing plan can have a tremendously positive impact on your firm. First, it helps the organization cope with change more rapidly and effectively, particularly through the use of contingency plans. Contingency plans offer alternative strategies should the initial strategy prove inadequate.

Second, the marketing plan helps an organization update and revise company objectives. If in some unforeseen circumstances the objectives cannot be achieved, the marketing plan can help a firm determine why the original goals could not be met and enable them to revise objectives and strategies quickly.

Third, establishing a marketing plan aids management decision making. The plan can serve as a point of reference for weighing alternative choices and determining which will contribute the most to meeting company objectives.

Fourth, the development of short-range and long-range marketing plans can help management evaluate marketing efforts. Actual results can be compared against projected results. In this way, management can establish control and measurement procedures for the marketing process and determine how well it achieves its objectives.

Pitfalls in Market Planning

Establishing a marketing plan or detailed strategic plans is not without potential hazards. While the benefits far outweigh the drawbacks, you should be aware of some common pitfalls in your planning process.

First, defining objectives and formulating a marketing plan is time-consuming. The time that management invests in the planning activity can be expensive. The results must justify that expense. Normally, the benefits of these efforts more than make up for the cost to the company.

Second, if the plan is poorly or hastily conceived or is based on erroneous assumptions or data, the outcome can be financially disastrous. In addition, such a plan cannot be adjusted effectively to changing conditions or unexpected events. Planning cannot compensate for poor research, nor can it take all of the risk out of doing business. But it will give you more information for decision making and control and reduce the level of uncertainty about the decisions you make.

Third, some plans fail because they are not integrated into the daily activities of the marketing function. The best plan is worthless if it sits on the shelf in the manager's office. Marketing plans should be implemented, evaluated, revised, and implemented again. Also, the effectiveness of a plan does not depend on its length. You should create a plan that is concise and to the point. The longer the plan, the less likely it will be read and used.

Fourth, the planning process may not be understood by the planners. The plan must be developed step by step, as we do in this book. Many managers are tempted to skip steps or to draw conclusions before they have adequate data. Every member of the planning team should understand each step and contribute to completing it.

Fifth, nonmarketing managers often are not asked to provide input into the plan. The marketing plan will be implemented in part by managers of departments removed from the marketing function. Without their input and support, the possibility of failure increases. The final plan must be accepted by all managers.

Sixth, financial projections may be mistakenly regarded as planning. Projections by themselves are not plans; they only forecast sales. Planning takes place when strategies for achieving sales projections are clearly defined.

Seventh, plans can fall through when planners fail to gather adequate data or consider the major variables the environment may present. While it is impossible to know all the variables, having too little information is a real danger. Managers may form conclusions or decide on strategies too quickly and make serious errors in judgment. Gathering sufficient, quality data is a critical part of good planning.

Finally, when too much focus is placed on short-term results, the firm can quickly outgrow the plan. Emphasis should be on developing plans that define long-term goals for company growth. Too often, companies sacrifice long-range profits for short-term results. The marketing plan by design should be flexible enough to accommodate short-term and long-range goals.

Take time to work carefully through the planning steps presented in this book. The guidelines we have developed can help you to minimize the hazards of planning and enable you to build a sound, future-oriented marketing plan.

Marketing Plan Outline

Starting with Chapter 2, we will take you systematically through the market planning process. The basic components of creating a marketing plan are shown in Figure 1.3. In the following chapters, we discuss each of the steps listed and provide questionnaires, matrices, and charts to help you gather and analyze the data you need.

The marketing plan outline follows the planning process we have discussed in this chapter. It begins with the overall company mission

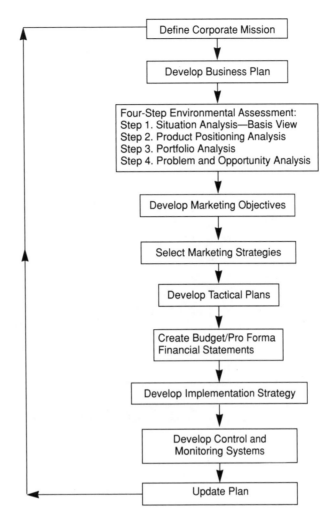

Figure 1.3 Steps in Developing a Marketing Plan

and business plan, which has established company-wide objectives and strategies.

The next steps involve analyzing the internal and external environments and developing marketing objectives and strategies. You then select the best strategies and develop procedures to implement and communicate the plans. The last step is to establish control mechanisms to measure results and monitor overall progress toward meeting company goals. This in turn leads back to the beginning of the cycle—making adjustments to the company mission statement.

At the end of the book you will have a considerable body of information with which to develop your marketing plan. The plan can serve as the blueprint for your company's growth and as a guide for its future success.

Summary

- Marketing can be defined broadly as the function within a company that seeks to generate a profit by organizing the firm's resources and activities to determine and satisfy the needs and desires of consumers. Marketing is considered a management function and emphasizes increased profits, not merely sales.

- The marketing concept is a management philosophy that states the key task of the company is to discover what various target markets want and need and to deliver the desired products and services more effectively and efficiently than the competition does.

- Keys to a successful planning process include these: (1) management must see the need for change; (2) someone or some group must champion the strategic market planning process; (3) the planning process must have high credibility with all levels of management and all users; (4) managers and staff should be trained in procedures essential to the planning process; and (5) written plans must be concise and well organized.

- The planning process begins with the company mission statement, which defines what the firm is, what business it is in, and what its broad-range goals are.

- The mission statement is translated into a set of objectives that serve as the basis for the business plan. Strategies then determine the overall design or program for achieving objectives.

- The company planning cycle includes a hierarchy of plans: business plan, marketing plan, and product plans.

- The business plan spells out the current status of a company's business and the direction in which the company is headed. It is influenced by input from the marketing and product plans as they are developed and implemented.

- The marketing plan can be thought of as the company's blueprint for future growth and success and serves as the major link between the business firm and its environment. It defines goals, procedures, and methods that will determine the company's future.

- Product plans are used to analyze product performance and establish product objectives, strategies, and tactics aimed at meeting the overall marketing plan strategies. Product plans provide ways to determine profit and derivation of net profit.

- The market planning cycle is driven by consumer needs and wants. It is designed to develop a proactive rather than reactive plan.

- Benefits of a good marketing plan include helping the organization to cope more rapidly and effectively with change, to update and revise company objectives, to aid management decision making, and to evaluate marketing efforts.

- Several pitfalls and hazards of market planning should be recognized: (1) the process is time consuming; the results must justify the cost; (2) a poorly conceived plan can produce disastrous results; (3) plans may not be integrated into the daily activities of the firm; (4) the planners may not fully understand the process; (5) nonmarketing managers may be left out of the process; (6) financial projections may be regarded as planning; (7) planners may fail to gather adequate data or consider key variables in the environment; and (8) if too much focus is placed on short-term results, the firm can quickly outgrow the plan.

Sample Case   DataStar*

DataStar is a medium-sized office equipment firm in the Midwest, once considered one of the "up and comers" in its field. In the past several years, however, the firm has watched its overall sales and market share steadily decline.

The sales manager at DataStar had been responsible for market planning but performed the function haphazardly. Top management realized that their engineering-oriented firm needed help in the marketing area. They created the position of Vice President of Marketing and, after an intensive search, hired Greg Haines, a market planning expert.

DataStar's problem is a familiar one to Haines, a problem he's seen in many companies that lack a formal, ongoing planning process. The firms rise or fall on a combination of product strength and lucky timing. DataStar originally entered the office electronics field at a time when competition was light. From management's point of view, there was little need for market planning.

Based on his experience with other companies, Haines knows he has his work cut out for him. His first step is to research DataStar's background and management history.

DataStar was founded in 1968 by three engineers—Howard Price, Sandra Koster, and Charles Simic—who left a major electronics corpo-

*The company DataStar, its management, products, and all marketing data are purely hypothetical. Any resemblance to any actual firm, persons, or situations is strictly coincidental.

ration to form their own company. They fit the profile of many entrepreneurs: strong in technical expertise and well connected with suppliers in the industry but weak in financial and marketing strategy. Price is the only one who attempts any type of formal planning work; he develops the company's Business Plan each year. Koster and Simic are more interested in product development, while Simic is openly skeptical about the value of marketing plans in general.

The three founders own 51 percent of the company's outstanding stock and are considered partners by other members of the firm. Howard Price is the firm President, Sandra Koster is Vice President of Engineering, and Charles Simic is Vice President of Operations/Research and Development. Top management also includes vice president of finance and the sales manager.

DataStar originally offered electric typewriters, adding machines, and other office equipment as its major product line. Since 1978, however, the company has been moving into automated equipment and supplies, developing its own computer peripheral devices and software in addition to its own line of products. The company currently has seven product lines: typewriters, adding machines and calculators, business forms, computer cable equipment, office products and furniture, computer peripherals, and software. Computer peripherals have the largest impact on sales, contributing 28 percent of total revenues.

The company has been considered a high-growth firm in a high-growth industry, with several locations across the country. In the past, management has developed new products primarily through acquisitions. The company's overall capital structure is sound. Customers view DataStar's products as high-quality items, and the company's excellent customer services have made it one of the most respected companies in the market.

However, the office automation industry has become intensely competitive since DataStar first entered the field. Major market leaders have established their product lines, and other companies must adapt their product offerings to the leaders' equipment.

DataStar has identified small to medium-sized firms as its target market and has concentrated on reaching these companies with its promotions and advertising. Until recently, they've done well. The company's sales have climbed from $24 million to more than $120 million in the past eleven years. But over the past three years, growth rate of sales has declined substantially.

Eight months ago they acquired a new hard disk drive—AutoDrive—by purchasing a small company. They also acquired a patent for storing all data from mainframes to the hard disks used in many mini- and microcomputers. For the past four months, AutoDrive has been sold only to select Midwest customers. Then one month ago, DataStar began offering AutoDrive throughout their Midwest territory.

Now the partners want to launch AutoDrive on the national market within the next twelve months. But the sales and service staffs are only trained to handle the new product in the Midwest. Haines can see that the acquisition and offering of AutoDrive has been haphazard. The company has no real objectives, strategies, or tactics for marketing the product. This reinforces Haines's evaluation that DataStar lacks any market planning process. He wants to monitor AutoDrive carefully, because this is the company's only new product and it has considerable sales potential.

As Haines continued his research, he pinpointed a number of other major problems.

• Although DataStar has been number one in its niche for several years, it is no longer considered a leading-edge company by its customers and competitors. Its early successes have come more from being first in the market with a quality product rather than as the result of a strategic plan. As the competition catches up, DataStar has no strategy for staying ahead.

• The primary reason for the change in position is the fact that Price, Koster, and Simic have become reactive rather than proactive managers. Two clear indications of the shift are these:

1. DataStar is milking its big revenue-producer product line dry without developing plans to regenerate products or keep up with changing technology. Fewer new products have been coming out of the R & D department.

2. When strategic decisions about DataStar's future need to be made, top management prefer to take a conservative line and follow competitors' leads. As a result, DataStar has lost the initiative in several product areas.

• Departments show a noticeable lack of communication and cohesiveness. Morale is low, and workers feel a general lack of leadership from top management.

• The marketing department, which has an effective team, has been following a "push" strategy rather than a "pull" strategy for product promotion and distribution. As a result, the marketing team is not identifying new customer groups nor evaluating sales data to pinpoint product strengths and weaknesses in the marketplace.

• While Price develops a Business Plan each year, it is never implemented. Price creates the plan in a vacuum without input from department heads, and he has no strategy for introducing and implementing his objectives. Nevertheless, Haines feels that he can use Price's Business Plan as a starting point to make the company more marketing oriented.

Looking over the problems he had uncovered, Haines knew that to get the company moving would mean making changes in the corporate culture. Since he was the new man on the team, introducing these changes would require some strategic planning of its own. He would need all of his diplomatic and communication skills to persuade top management that they must alter some of their old ways of doing business.

He began by volunteering to work with Price on the Business Plan to increase the marketing department's responsibilities in the firm. Price was more than willing to share what had become a thankless job.

"I've been putting this plan together for seven years, and no one has ever used it," Price lamented.

"We need to get all department heads involved in the planning process from the start," Haines insisted. "They should be providing information and reviewing the plan at each step. Even before we begin data gathering, however, we need to establish a sound mission statement. What does your current statement say?"

Price sorted through his papers and found the statement. It read:

The purpose of DataStar is to be a leading supplier of typewriters and other office equipment.

Haines saw immediately that the statement's short-sighted focus was one of the obstacles to company growth; DataStar needed a new, expanded mission statement. Haines persuaded Price to call a top management meeting to develop it. In particular, the three partners had to answer some critical questions. Who are we as a company? What business are we in? Who are our customers? After considerable deliberation, management defined a new mission for the firm.

Form 1   Mission Statement

The purpose of DataStar is to provide the highest quality service and office automation products to our customers through our core business and new ventures so that our share of the market is strengthened, our employees and business partners benefit from our success, and shareholders receive a superior return on their investment.

The statement was brief but specific about the arena in which the company would compete and at what level. The first statement was much more narrow and limited. The new statement reflected not only the shift in product line but also a goal to gain a solid share of this market. Its open-ended expression didn't constrain or limit the company's growth.

During the process of developing the statement, top management realized that they had to make changes in the company to achieve its mission. As Vice President of Marketing, Haines would be the one to champion the use of strategic market planning and to raise the level of marketing expertise.

"I think it should be clear," Haines told the management group, "that for any real change to succeed, the planning process has to have top management backing and involve all levels of management and users. Otherwise, it's just another plan no one will read or implement."

The three partners agreed to give Haines their full support. Koster quickly saw the value of introducing a company-wide planning process. "I think in the past we expected that just developing a plan would make things happen. Howard has been doing the whole job on his own."

Haines said, "It's plain from the sales figures that the company can't rest on its reputation; nor do you want to become just an order-taking firm. Too many other companies are entering this market, and fast. On top of that, technology in this field is changing so rapidly that unless we take the initiative, your customers are going to see you as lagging behind the competition."

Simic, the most skeptical about the entire marketing approach, broke in. "Just exactly how are you going to get this whole planning process going? The way you talk we don't have much time, especially since we're planning to launch AutoDrive nationally this year."

Haines agreed. "The first step is to find out where we stand right now and get some idea of where the firm's current policies will take us in, say, three years. That means collecting a lot of data, both internal and external. That's why it's crucial we have the cooperation of all departments."

Haines held up the completed mission statement. "We've already taken the first step. The mission statement is the foundation for the Business Plan. Howard Price and I have reviewed the current Business Plan and identified some missing pieces."

Haines explained that DataStar's Business Plan objectives failed to include all departments and were generally too narrow, focusing on specific products, for example, rather than on product lines. Second, the objectives often were blue-sky items—not reasonable, obtainable, or measurable. Third, the plan included the tactical level but should have stayed at the strategic level.

Finally, the Business Plan was more than 700 pages long. No one around the management table had ever read through the document nor had any intention of following it. Because Price had worked by himself on the plan, it was only as good as his knowledge of the internal and external environment. In some areas, Price admitted he had rather sketchy information.

Haines outlined the planning process: "The Business Plan objectives must provide direction for the company. What product lines do we want to develop? What markets do we want to enter?

"These business strategies in turn become the objectives for each department. And each department works out their own strategies and the tactics to achieve them. The marketing plan coordinates all these departmental strategies and acts as the major link between the firm and its internal and external environment."

But Haines made it clear that the success of a new strategic marketing plan depended on two key factors:

- Level of commitment from all those persons involved in the planning process.
- Degree to which the plan keeps up with changes in the market environment.

"I realize we're talking about a lot of work at the beginning, but believe me, the results are worth it. We'll have a marketing plan that explains what's to be done, where it's to be done, and who is to do each job. The plan stresses a team approach to achieve our goals, and that can boost morale and make working together easier and more productive.

"DataStar will be able to respond faster to competitive challenges and marketplace changes; and in this field, that can make all the difference. You'll have more reliable data at your fingertips and contingency plans to choose from. And we'll have some yardsticks for evaluating our marketing efforts, rather than using a hit-or-miss method."

Koster and Price were enthusiastic about the process, and even Simic seemed resigned to it. "I guess it's either learn this marketing approach," Simic said, "or lose our company."

PART TWO

Environmental Assessment

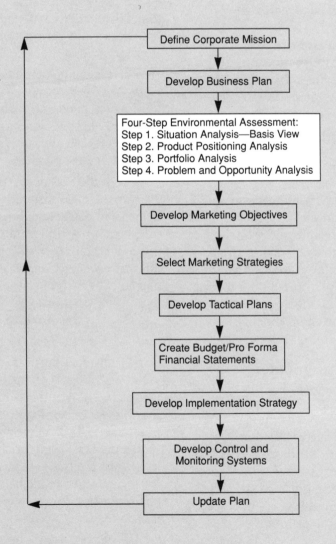

Define Corporate Mission

Develop Business Plan

Four-Step Environmental Assessment:
Step 1. Situation Analysis—Basis View
Step 2. Product Positioning Analysis
Step 3. Portfolio Analysis
Step 4. Problem and Opportunity Analysis

Develop Marketing Objectives

Select Marketing Strategies

Develop Tactical Plans

Create Budget/Pro Forma
Financial Statements

Develop Implementation Strategy

Develop Control and
Monitoring Systems

Update Plan

An environmental assessment is similar to a marketing audit, but it looks at an organization's internal and external environment from a broader perspective. The assessment involves analyzing major internal and external factors that affect your firm and anticipating what these factors are likely to be in the near future. Will they change or remain the same? Do you anticipate new factors arising?

The environmental assessment is a proactive rather than reactive tool. It can help you to anticipate problems and opportunities rather than react to them after they happen. Such an analysis focuses on decisions that must be made *today* to eliminate or minimize threats and to maximize opportunities.

You can use the environmental assessment to build a clear picture of the real world in which your firm operates and estimate how that world is likely to change. This process should not be considered an academic exercise performed once a year. Instead it must be an ongoing process that helps to forecast the environmental situation throughout your planning cycle.

Four-Step Environmental Assessment Process

The environmental assessment is completed in four stages: situation analysis—basis view, product positioning evaluation, product portfolio analysis, and problem and opportunity analysis. As shown in Figure 2.A, the assessment leads to the next step in the planning process: setting marketing objectives and selecting appropriate strategies for your organization. To help you gain the greatest benefit from the environmental assessment, we go through the process in the following sequence:

Step 1. Situation analysis—basis view—(Chapter 2). In this step we use a *qualitative* approach to discuss general environmental issues affecting your firm and to ask questions that stimulate your thinking and determine voids in the knowledge and information available for decision making.

Step 2. Product positioning—micro view—(Chapter 3). We take the qualitative information generated from the basis view and use a questionnaire approach to *quantify* certain areas according to your firm's individual products.

Data from the questionnaires in steps 1 and 2 are applied and mapped on various matrices to determine the current and three-year projected position of each product within its environment. We introduce strategic gap analysis in this chapter.

The micro view is excellent for determining individual product strategies and tactics to reposition products in the future.

Step 3. Product portfolio analysis—macro view—(Chapter 4). In this step we take all the micro views and combine them into a macro view or portfolio of the entire product line for the current and three-year projected view. Portfolio analysis is critical to support the business plan and to develop the strategic marketing plan. It identifies characteristics, strengths, weaknesses, and gaps in the total product line.

Step 4. Problem and opportunity analysis—(Chapter 5). This step examines the data developed in the questionnaires

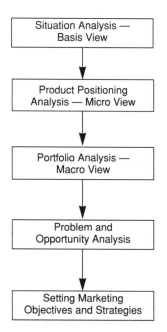

Figure 2.A
Data Flow from the Environmental Assessment

and matrices to help you pinpoint potential problems and opportunities. Some will be obvious, others less so. The point is to identify them now so that action steps can be designed and included as part of the marketing plan.

It is critical that your environmental assessment follow this systematic approach. Each step is built on data gathered in the step before it. If you skip steps, your environmental picture will be incomplete, and you will have less reliable data for selecting your marketing objectives and strategies.

An Ongoing Process

The environmental assessment will help to prioritize the areas that require the most attention. You may need to know more about your competitive situation, for example, or how to change your pricing structure. After completing the assessment, you will be able to develop sound objectives and strategies.

The value of maintaining an ongoing environmental analysis is that over time your data become more refined and reliable. You learn to apply more sophisticated modeling techniques as you gain experience. The approach we have taken in this book provides a framework and systematic method of evaluating individual products and services, product lines, and subsidiary businesses. You can adapt any part of this approach for your own company.

The main point in conducting an environmental assessment is to understand your organization and the internal/external environment in which it operates. Once this point is understood by managers and staff, you are well on your way to developing a sound strategic marketing plan.

CHAPTER TWO

Step 1: Situation Analysis—Basis View

Introduction

In this chapter we begin the first stage of gathering data for your strategic marketing plan. The foundation of a solid plan is a reliable set of basic data.

Our purpose is to stimulate your thinking about various internal and external factors that affect your firm and the products and services it offers. This approach can help you to spot emerging threats and opportunities arising from changes in the business environment.

Keep in mind that we are focusing on the broad picture in this step rather than gathering detailed information about each environmental factor. Such a detailed analysis begins in the following chapters, 3 through 5. For now, you need to understand the general strengths and voids in your knowledge base regarding your organization and its operating environment. This approach gives you some idea of what research you need to do to fill in those voids.

Importance of the Analysis

To those who have never undertaken an environmental assessment, the process may seem unnecessary or too elementary. Some managers believe that because they have been involved with their company for a number of years they know where it stands and in which direction it should go. To them, an internal/external analysis is superfluous.

Nothing could be further from the truth. Although this assessment takes time to conduct, it is essential to generate valuable marketing data on which to base strategic decisions. If the analysis is incomplete or inadequate, the entire plan will suffer.

As you work through the first step—basis view—of the environmental analysis, you will find that not all factors discussed can be quantified on some type of objective scale. You may have to rely on your experience and on the experience of other managers and staff to evaluate certain factors.

If you manufacture robotic toys, for example, what types of computerized or programmable toys will attract consumers next year? Although you can conduct market research on consumer preferences, needs, and past buying patterns, the answer may still be difficult to pin down. Marketing managers, in the final analysis, may have to make decisions based on their own intuition regarding which way the consumer is likely to jump in the coming season.

Emphasizing Qualitative Data

We will not focus on *quantitative* data at this point but will concentrate on *qualitative* data regarding demand, competition, cost structure, and so on. The questions we ask in this chapter are not meant to be answered in detail right away but to prepare you for more quantitative work in later chapters. However, these questions *will* need to be answered in-depth as you work through the book.

Remember, the purpose of this step is discovery, to discover what you do and don't know about your company and the environment in which you do business. Form 2: Assessing the Competition will help you to evaluate your situation. Use the questionnaire as a research tool. It is not a judgment of anyone's ability or knowledge but simply a means of discovering what is known and unknown about the company's overall situation. Successful companies spend considerable time and money discovering their weak points as well as developing their strengths.

Basis View

Understanding the total business environment in which a firm competes is basic to market planning. The environment determines not only what a firm must do to thrive and grow, but what it is possible for the firm to do.

The basis view covers three areas:

1. External factors: General market conditions in which the organization operates and over which it has little control. We focus on three critical areas: demand, competition, and economic climate.

2. Internal factors: General conditions within the organization over which it has control. In this section we concentrate primarily on the key areas of personnel skills and financial resources.

3. Internal/external factors: These include influences from within and outside your firm that impact its performance and success. Some can be controlled by management while others cannot. We focus on life cycle analysis for the industry, your company, and your products; cost structure; legal constraints; and distribution channels.

The variables we list in each section are the minimum number that should be considered either quantitatively or qualitatively for developing a marketing plan. If you have other variables important to your firm, add them to the list. If some of the variables do not fit your company, delete them and add those factors that do fit your organization and its environment.

After each variable, we ask a series of questions. Note any questions that you and other managers in the firm cannot answer. Briefly assess how the lack of data will increase the level of uncertainty and risk in developing strategies. You will also realize at this point how much research is needed to fill in the data voids these questions reveal.

External Factors

External factors are those that impact the firm from outside over which you have little control—demand, competition, economic climate. We define the terms used because they may have different meanings to different individuals, and clarity is essential as the analysis progresses.

You need to develop as complete an understanding as possible of these variables and their effects on your organization. The success of your marketing plan hinges largely on how well you estimate their influence.

Demand. Demand is the single most significant situational variable because it has the greatest impact on what the firm can or cannot do. At the same time it is one of the more difficult factors to determine and predict.

Demand is usually defined as the number of units of a particular product or service that customers wish to purchase over a specific time and under a particular set of conditions. Demand for a product can be affected by several factors:

- Consumers' income levels.
- Price and availability of competitors' goods.
- Appearance of superior substitute products.
- Advertising efforts.
- Economic trends.

Any firm that wants to survive in the marketplace must have a basic understanding of the demand for their products and services. The demand estimate drives the revenue forecast that serves as the basis for determining the advertising program, production schedules, product enhancements, inventories, capital expenditures, number of staff required, and so on.

When analyzing the demand for your products, you will need to answer the following questions:

- What is the current size of the market in units or dollars, and what will it be in the future?
- What is the extent of demand for the firm's products or services?
- What is the nature of that demand—seasonal, year-round, fluctuating, weak, strong?
- How do consumers buy existing products or services?
- What are consumers' basic behavior patterns and attitudes?
- Can the market be segmented into homogeneous groups on the basis of types of products or services bought and consumer behavior?
- Is it best to analyze the market as a whole or as various segments?
- Should a separate marketing program be developed for each segment? If so, what are the requirements for success in each market segment?

You can obtain information on the nature of demand for your products, the size of the market, and consumer behavior by conducting market research yourself, by hiring a marketing firm to do parts of the research for you, and by collecting the information from available sources. These sources include industry surveys, reports of private market research firms, government studies, and association surveys and studies.

Competition. Understanding your competitive situation is the second most critical element in your environmental assessment. Without this information, you will not be able to develop a successful marketing plan. If competition is intense, you will need a different marketing program than if it is moderate.

Competition among firms can be either *direct* (another company is in the same market area) or *indirect* (a mail order firm offers a line of products similar to yours) and is based only partly on price. Nonprice factors can be just as important to customers. They include service, product differentiation, quality, and support services.

Most firms, while aware of their direct and indirect competition, fail to consider the potential threat from new entrants into the market

Most firms, while aware of their direct and indirect competition, fail to consider the potential threat from new entrants into the market or the expansion strategies of current or future competitors. You should be aware that newcomers can enter your market from one of several starting points:

- The new firm plans to enter through diversification.

- The new firm offers products and services identical to yours and is planning to expand into your market from other customer markets in which it operates.

- The new firm currently offers a limited product line to customers in your area but is planning to expand its offerings to include products or services you now offer.

- The new firm decides to use forward integration to gain entry into your market.

Analyzing possible threats from newcomers and the expansion threats of others in your area is one part of understanding your competitive situation.

To analyze direct and indirect competition, consider the following questions:

1. What is the current strategy of your competition?

Although this information is generally not easy to obtain, you can make some educated estimates about competitor strategy by observing their marketing programs, through secondary research, and by looking at their past product history. Gaining market intelligence should be a top priority of the company. Consider these questions:

- How do they define their missions?

- Are their companies being managed for sales, growth, market share, net income, return on investment, cash flow?

- How vertically integrated are they?

- How have they defined their business in terms of customer groups, customer functions, and technology?

- What is their marketing mix, manufacturing policy, purchasing policy, physical distribution policy?

- What size are their budgets and how are they allocated?

- To what extent are they affecting your company's growth rate, market share, profitability?

- What is the present and future structure of competition?

2. How are your competitors performing?

Actual performance should be determined as closely as possible in terms of sales, growth, market share, profit margins, net income, and return on investment (ROI).

3. What are competitors' strengths and weaknesses?

An analysis of competitors' strengths and weaknesses should include a comparative assessment of factors such as the following:

- Product and product quality.
- Dealers and distribution channels.
- Marketing and selling capabilities.
- Operations and physical distribution.
- Financial capabilities—resources and outlay.
- Costs and how costs are changing.

4. What action can be expected from them in the future?

You need to have some idea how your competitors are likely to respond in the near future to changes in the industry. You will need to answer the following questions:

- How are they likely to respond to ongoing changes in the external environment?
- How are they likely to respond to specific competitor moves?
- When and where are they most vulnerable?
- When and where are they strongest?
- In what markets are they most vulnerable to your competitive programs?
- How can you best fight them in these and other markets?

The more complete your understanding of the competitive picture is, the more successful you will be in designing a marketing strategy.

Environmental Economic Climate. Besides demand and the competitive situation, you must also gain some perspective on the overall economic climate in which you do business. Marketing programs can be easily disrupted by changing economic conditions. Many firms were caught by surprise when OPEC initiated an oil embargo in the 1970s. Likewise, the high interest rates of the late 1970s and early 1980s hurt the profitability of many companies, while declines in consumer disposable income hurt such leisure businesses as the travel and entertainment industry.

Since economic conditions are constantly changing, you will need to consider how your firm can adapt to change for long-term success. You should answer some of these questions:

- What are the social, political, economic, and technological trends occurring now and those likely to occur in the next one to three years?

- How do you evaluate these trends in terms of their impact on your industry and your firm?

- Do these trends represent opportunities or threats?

- How are basic economic conditions affecting sales and other functions of the firm? How are they likely to affect your firm in the next one to three years?

Information on economic conditions can be obtained from a variety of sources including government studies and surveys, Federal Reserve Bank bulletins, industry reports and seminars, private forecasting and research firms, industry publications, and your research.

Internal Factors

Internal factors are those that affect the company from the inside and can be controlled more directly by the firm. The principal internal factors to consider are your company's personnel and financial resources. You may also add other factors such as management leadership, company image, and organizational structure.

Personnel Skills. Part of the market planning process involves evaluating the skills and experience of your company's employees. You want to make sure that you have adequate staff to carry out the goals you set for your firm. Employees must also have the necessary level of skills to perform the work.

For example, you plan to increase sales by 25 percent over the next two years. Do you have enough staff with the required skills to explore new markets, increase the size of your sales territory, add service accounts?

Your evaluation should gather the following information:

- What types of skills and experience will you need to accomplish your corporate goals and mission in the next three to five years?

- Does the firm possess the skills and experience needed to operate successfully in this business?

- Do you have the number of skilled staff required to accomplish your projected goals?

- How do your skills compare with those of your competitors?

- What training programs will you need to upgrade the skills of your current staff?

- What are the cost differentials of hiring skilled people versus upgrading the skills of your present staff?

A careful audit of personnel is essential to any marketing plan.

Financial Resources. You will also need to audit your financial resources to determine whether you have sufficient capital to finance your marketing plan. Resources include cash flow from operations, real estate earnings, potential stock and bond offerings, inventory, cash, accounts receivable, available lines of credit, and other sources you may be able to tap.

Evaluate your financial resources using the following questions as a guide:

- Do you have the funds to support an effective marketing program?
- Can you finance your growth objectives, e.g., purchasing additional facilities, adding onto the present plant, acquiring other businesses, expanding into new markets, developing new products?
- From where are the funds coming, and when will they be available?
- Do you have sufficient financial resources to expand internally and externally without hurting the overall health of the corporation?
- What types of financing structure can you afford? What is the optimal capital structure?
- What rate of return on your investment can you expect and over what time period? What profit margins do you anticipate or need?
- Are there any accounts receivable problems?
- Is the total volume of revenue increasing or decreasing? Are revenues fluctuating, and if so, why?
- What do the pro forma statements look like under various financial scenarios?

Accurate estimates of financial resources are critical. Many marketing plans fail because firms overextend themselves financially and cannot follow through on their goals. They run out of capital before they begin to see any substantial return on their investment. On the other hand, an organization may grow too rapidly and become cash poor, resulting in operating losses and, in some cases, bankruptcy. Make sure your financial resources are able to support your marketing strategy.

Evaluate the other internal factors mentioned—management leadership, organizational structure, company image, and any others you feel are important. What is the current state of these factors, what will your needs be in one to three years, and what do you need to do to bring about any required changes?

Internal/External Factors

These factors include influences from both outside and within the firm that affect its performance and success. In this section we focus on a life cycle analysis of the industry, your organization, and your firm's products; cost structure; legal constraints; and distribution channels. Life cycle analysis provides a framework in which to develop your strategic marketing plan and to select appropriate strategies. It is one of the most useful and powerful concepts in market planning.

Life Cycle Analysis. As with the human life cycle, industries, organizations, and products generally follow four distinct stages: Introduction, Growth, Maturity, and Decline. Each stage of a life cycle has its own characteristics and applicable strategies. As shown in Figure 2.1, the industry life cycle exerts pressure on the organizational life cycle, which in turn affects single product life cycles. Since a change in any of these cycles has a direct influence on the others, it is important to understand this concept and how it affects your strategy development.

Industry Life Cycle. The industry life cycle has a direct bearing on the organizations and products that make up the industry. For example, if the industry is in a Growth Stage, there will be opportunities

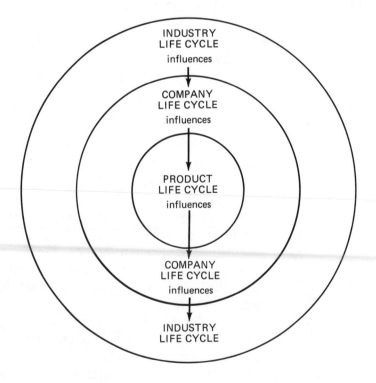

Figure 2.1 Life Cycle Analysis

for firms to expand. If the industry is in decline, however, companies within that industry will also decline unless they are able to diversify their product lines into other growth industries or can find profitable niches in the declining market.

Most industries in the United States are in their Mature Stage. Their growth rates are slow, and most of the markets are saturated, although they have enough new product innovations to keep the markets slowly expanding. However, if the structure of an industry changes—from regulated to deregulated, for example—the industry moves to a different stage in its life cycle.

This change happened in the trucking industry after it was deregulated in 1980. Before the change, the industry was in a stagnant Mature Stage; and most of the carriers had clearly defined market shares. After deregulation, the industry was suddenly thrown back into a Growth Stage. Most firms had no real understanding of how to compete in a deregulated market and continued to operate in the old way.

The result: many of the firms went bankrupt or merged with other companies. Although many companies knew that deregulation was coming, they did little or no strategic planning to handle the new situation. Companies could only react using crisis management tactics to try to stay in business.

An understanding of the industry life cycle and its implications is necessary to develop the proactive strategies that organizations need to remain competitive and growth oriented.

Organization Life Cycle.   At the next level, companies also have life cycles marked by definitive stages. A new software company, for example, in the Introduction Stage struggles to make itself known to consumers and to establish its market position with its products and services. In the Growth Stage, it gains customer acceptance and experiences a period of rapid growth and expansion.

During the Mature Stage, it reaches its peak output and efficiency. Revenues have stabilized and start to decline. The company must evaluate its position carefully and decide on a course of action. Should it expand some products, cut back on others, diversify, redefine its mission, merge with another firm? The strategy selected can make the difference between an extended Mature Stage, or even revitalized Growth Stage, versus a continued decline in revenues.

If the decrease in sales and revenues is not halted, the company enters a Decline Stage and faces several other alternatives. It may slowly lose market share until it goes out of business, settle on a reduced market share, or sell its operation to another firm.

Product Life Cycle.   Each product has a definite life cycle marking its development, entry into the market, maturity, and decline, as

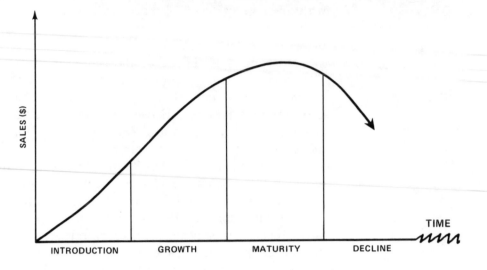

Figure 2.2 Product Life Cycle

shown in Figure 2.2. Since product life cycles are discussed in more detail in Chapters 6 and 7, we give only a brief introduction to each phase here.

It is important to know which stage your products have reached in their life cycle as you begin your planning process. This knowledge will help you determine the next stage your products are likely to enter in the near future, given your current strategy. It will also help you to decide on any new strategies you may need to maximize your market share, revenue, and profitability.

In the Introduction Stage, the product is placed on the market and begins to generate revenue. Competition for new products is often negligible since this stage usually yields little or no profit. The marketing strategy is usually to gain consumer acceptance and make the product known.

In the Growth Stage, consumers become increasingly aware of the product. Demand rises and sales increase. Brand loyalty among consumers may develop. Competition is the most intense at this stage. The marketing strategy may include targeting more consumer groups and refining the product to satisfy customer desires.

In the Mature Stage, definite markets have been established, sales peak and begin to decline, competition stabilizes, few if any new entrants are expected, and market shares are relatively stable. Market share may increase if the brand gains added value through product improvements or price restructuring. Marketing strategies usually focus on maintaining market share with consideration of what the organization will do when the product reaches the Decline Stage.

At the end of the cycle, the Decline Stage, revenue drops off rapidly, new technology or changed conditions in the market begin to make the product obsolete, competition declines as competitors drop out of the market, and the product is displaced or repositioned to an earlier stage. The marketing strategy is designed to minimize losses and to discontinue or reposition the product as quickly as possible.

When you analyze your products and services more closely in Chapters 3 and 4, you will answer questions such as these:

- What is the life cycle stage of each product or product line?

- What is the organizational life cycle of your company?

- What is the life cycle stage of your industry?

- What market data support your evaluation?

Cost Structure of the Industry.   The cost structure of an industry is important to profit margins, competitive vulnerability, and pricing or how a firm establishes the price of a product or service. Whatever affects the cost structure will have a direct impact on a company's pricing, profits, and current strategies.

You need to know the current cost structure and the changes that are likely to occur in that structure in the near future. The added cost of supplying more products or services to consumers helps to determine the marketing program that your firm should follow.

Questions you will need to answer include these:

- What is the current cost structure in the industry?

- Can you operate profitably within that structure?

- Can the current cost structure be changed? How?

- If costs increase, how will your firm's pricing and profit margin be affected?

- Do your competitors possess any cost advantages over your firm? What is the advantage and how can you counteract it?

- Can competitors cross-subsidize products to achieve a short-range price advantage over you?

Legal Constraints.   Legal constraints can affect either the external or internal environment of your firm. A desirable marketing plan may be hampered by antitrust laws, pricing restraints, interstate commerce restrictions, rulings on what constitutes fair competition, and deregulation of an industry.

The legal environment is constantly changing. You must design your marketing program within this legal framework. To do so means you must monitor the latest legal developments and assess their impact on your firm and the industry. You will need to answer questions such as these:

- How can you stay informed of legal changes in order to anticipate problems or opportunities that may exist?
- Are your marketing programs within the legal limits?
- How do current or proposed regulations affect the firm in terms of competitive stance, plans for acquisition or divestiture, pricing structure?
- What new or proposed legislation is pending at the city, state, or federal level that may affect your firm?
- How should you adjust your marketing plans and programs to respond to legislative changes?

You can gather information on the legal climate from a number of sources: government legislative publications, industry lobbying groups, your legislators, industry associations and seminars, business publications and professional journals, and your own legal department, if the firm is large enough to maintain this function.

Distribution Channels. Companies generally have some control over which channels will carry their products from plant to the end user. You may even own part of the distribution channel in the form of trucks, airlines, vans, ships, and other types of transportation.

For market planning purposes, you will need to answer the following questions:

- What distribution channels exist and how can your firm gain access to them?
- What major trends are emerging in distribution channel structure in the industry? What impact will these trends have on your organization in terms of delivery, price, cost, and revenue?
- How much competition exists within and among channels?
- What are the requirements of each channel for promotion and for margin?
- What are the costs versus revenue ratios for each channel?
- Which channels will be the most profitable for your firm to use?
- Are you using the best channels to minimize cost and maximize revenues? What changes should be made?

Assessing the Competition Questionnaire

Form 2: Assessing the Competition will help you to gather data about your major competitors for the basis view. Look over the completed form for the Sample Case, which indicates the information this questionnaire is designed to generate.

Purpose of the Form

The form covers six major areas in evaluating your major competitors and your company:

- Market segments.
- Product and service offerings.
- Company strengths and weaknesses.
- Strategies.
- Market shares.
- Distribution channels.

In answering questions about your products and those of the competition, you will also be generating data to be analyzed and used in the following chapters. In particular, the data will help you to fill out Form 3: Product Evaluation Questionnaire. In succeeding chapters, we will show you how to draw conclusions from the data you develop, what the data mean in relation to your company's particular situation, and how you can use this information to develop your strategic marketing plan.

Instructions for Completing the Form

Fill out a questionnaire for each product your company markets. Make sure that department heads and other pertinent staff members look over the completed form and make comments. The broader your data base, the more you are likely to learn.

The following instructions should help you complete the questionnaire.

1. Identify the market segment in which you do business and enter it at the top of the form. If you compete in more than one defined segment or market, fill out separate forms for each product offering.

2. Section A: Your Firm's Product Offering—List the product you offer in a particular segment. If you offer more than one product in a segment or market, fill out a separate form for each product. (These

forms will be correlated later to identify any overlap, to develop pricing structures, and so on.)

3. Section B: Competitor Products—After each of your products, list the competitor's products that compete most directly with yours.

It may be that a competitor's products cannot be associated with any of yours in the segment. You may want to list the competing product and assess it anyway, since that will give you a sense of the competitor's market coverage.

On the other hand, you may know of a competitor's product that competes with yours but be unable to assess it in any detail or with any degree of confidence. This would point out a void in your research. In that case, simply list the competing product and note that you could not assess it at this time.

4. Section C: Quantitative or Qualitative Judgments—Answer these questions about you and your competitors in the context of your respective situations. For example, in question C-15, if your product is strictly regulated in that segment, you would rate your own regulatory climate as "high." In contrast, if your competitor's product is relatively free from regulation, you would rate the competitor's regulatory climate as "low" for each product. Compared with your firm, the competitor enjoys a climate fairly free from restrictive regulation.

5. Section D: Competitor Information—Answer the questions in this section from the competitor's viewpoint, unless the question specifically asks you to compare the competitor's offering with your product.

Answer as many questions as you can. Where possible, research the questions you cannot answer. The more complete your form, the more data you have to develop a sound marketing plan.

Keep in mind, however, that finding out what you don't know is as critical as filling in what you do know. These voids point out where you are vulnerable to competition or market changes and reveal potential problems and opportunities.

In Chapter 3, Product Positioning, we move on to the second step in the environmental analysis—evaluating your market position, life cycle stage, and strategic gaps.

Summary

- The purpose of the basis view is to help you understand the general strengths and weaknesses in your knowledge base regarding your organization and its operating environment. This approach can help you to spot emerging threats and opportunities arising from changes in the business environment.

- This step concentrates on qualitative data about external, internal, and internal/external environmental factors rather than on quantitative data.

- External factors include demand, competition, and the economic climate.

- Internal factors focus on personnel skills and financial resources but also consider management leadership, company image, organizational structure, and other factors.

- Internal/external factors cover life cycle analysis, cost structure, legal constraints, and distribution channels.

- Life cycle analysis examines industry, company, and products in terms of four stages: Introduction, Growth, Maturity, and Decline. Different marketing strategies are selected for each life cycle stage.

Sample Case
"What You Don't Know . . . Can Be Valuable"

Once Greg Haines was given approval to initiate a strategic market planning process, his first step was to review all the company's current marketing information. Not surprisingly, he found considerable gaps in the data. Haines called a departmental meeting to explain what the marketing team would do over the next few weeks.

"We need first of all to find out where the company stands in relation to its internal and external environment. That means getting the highest quality data we can both from inside and outside the firm. The marketing plan will only be as sound as the data supporting it. We'll focus on qualitative data first, since we can gather that from department heads and product managers more quickly.

"I think you all understand the limitations of qualitative and quantitative data, so no one is going to assign any absolute value to the information we gather. The final marketing plan will consider management experience and judgment as well as the numbers and percentages they can give us. Right now we want to find out where we have solid information and where we have gaps."

Haines planned to pay particular attention to AutoDrive, Data-Star's new hard disk drive. It is the first leading-edge product the company has produced since the recent acquisitions. Although AutoDrive has been sold to selected Midwest customers, it will not be fully launched nationally until the new marketing plan is in place. The marketing team will also gather data for each product in all seven of the company's product lines.

Haines explained that the marketing team would first conduct a situation analysis of the company to develop a basis set of data.

"It's vital that we get a much more thorough understanding of all marketplace variables. To begin, I've developed a competitive assessment questionnaire that I'll hand out to all appropriate department heads and product managers. The answers will enable us to assess their knowledge of markets, products, competitors, and the like."

"How will you get them to fill it out?" one member of the marketing team asked. "They hardly ever returned any of the questionnaires we sent them before. In fact, only about a third of the managers even bothered to read them."

"This time top management will see to it that the forms are completed," Haines replied. "That's why I insisted on having their full support before we started the planning process."

Despite his assurances, the team members remained skeptical. Haines didn't mind; he was confident their attitude would change once the data started coming in. From then on they'd be too busy to doubt his methods.

He asked Price, Koster, and Simic to call a meeting of all department heads and product managers to explain the purpose of his questionnaire. Haines wanted to defuse any suspicions on the managers' part that the form was being used to weed out their ranks.

Price let the group know that the three partners were in agreement with the marketing vice president's approach. He then turned the meeting over to Haines.

Haines stood up in front of the group. "You'll find the questionnaire covers a lot of territory from price structure to competitive strategy. I realize that competitor information can be hard to come by, but do the best you can with it. The whole purpose of this form is to find out what we do and don't know. I want to stress that honesty is important in filling out the questionnaire. No one is being judged by their answers—this is purely a fact-finding mission."

One of the managers interrupted, "What if we can't find any information to come up with an answer?"

"Leave the question blank. That's an indication of where you need to do some research later on. Right now all you're concerned with is what you can or can't answer at this time. That's why I'm stressing honesty so much. Don't put down an answer just to look good. We don't need junk information; we need to know where everyone stands. Any questions?"

"Do we fill out one questionnaire for each product and for each of that product's competitors?"

"That's right."

A chorus of groans greeted his answer. Haines held up his hands until he got silence. "I know it sounds like a lot of work, and it's something no one does voluntarily. But the company's in trouble and going to be in a lot worse trouble if we don't turn it around. We've got to have a solid understanding of the total business environment in which we're competing. That information will serve as the basis for our strategic marketing plan. Look at it this way—the time you invest in these forms is time invested in your jobs and your future here at DataStar."

Haines could see his words hit home. Everyone had seen the latest sales and market share statistics. "All right, take the forms with you and let's have the completed questionnaires turned in to the marketing department one week from today."

After the managers left, Simic shook his head gloomily. "You won't get half of those forms back," he predicted.

A week later, to Simic's surprise, all but two of the managers had turned in their completed questionnaires. Haines saw his marketing team's morale pick up noticeably as they threw themselves into the task of analyzing the data. For the first time, he began to feel a momentum for change building in the company.

The results of the analysis yielded a few surprises. For one thing, Haines was concerned at the lack of detailed information the product managers provided about the competition. As shown on the first page of Form 2, respondents judged Competitor A as the strongest threat to AutoDrive and Competitor C as the weakest. (The remaining sample questionnaire has been completed for Competitor A only. In actual fact, a form would be filled out for each competitor.)

The product managers and their staffs had the most trouble filling in questions about Competitor A's required investment, marketing strategy, price structure, profit margins, market share, growth rate, and target market segments.

The answers showed Haines that DataStar's product managers were not keeping abreast of changes in the marketplace nor the impact of those changes on the company. Instead, they were concerned with meeting short-term objectives, which he began to suspect were set too low. It was another sign that the company was not marketing oriented.

On the other hand, Haines was pleased at the managers' high level of knowledge about their own products. It was obvious that information about the internal environment was not the problem. The managers, it was clear, needed to become more aware of the external environment.

Haines had his marketing team pinpoint all data gaps, then assigned a special research group to fill in the voids. The group would work with management and their staffs to develop the needed information. Haines gave the research team three weeks to report back with their findings.

Simic shook his head. "It'll take them six months," he said.

Form 2   Assessing the Competition

Competitor Names: ___A, B, C___   Date: _____

_____   Market/Product Manager: _____

_____

	AutoDrive	A	B	C	
SECTION A: Our Product	AutoDrive				
SECTION B: Competitor's Products		A	B	C	

SECTION C

	AutoDrive	A	B	C	
1. Effectiveness of distribution channels (High–Medium–Low)	H	H	H	L	
2. Product life cycle stage (I-G-M-D)	I	I	I	I	
3. Product differentiation from competitors' offerings (H–M–L)	NA				
4. Cyclicality of market segment (i.e., constant, seasonal, etc.)(H–M–L)	M	M	M	M	
5. Skills of the firms (all aspects) (H–M–L)	H	M	L	L	
6. Product quality/service levels perceived by customers (H–M–L)	H	M	M	L	
7. Flexibility of pricing structure (H–M–L)	H	NA	NA	NA	
8. Price competitiveness (H–M–L)	M	M	M	M	
9. Substitution threat from competitors (H–M–L)	L	M	M	M	
10. Barriers to entry (H–M–L)	M	M	M	M	
11. Barriers to exit (H–M–L)	L	L	L	L	
12. Variety of applications and features (H–M–L)	M	L	L	L	
13. Capability for economies of scale (H–M–L)	M	M	M	M	
14. Raw materials easy to obtain (H–M–L)	M	M	M	M	
15. Regulatory climate (H–M–L)	M	M	M	M	

16. Risk in market segment (H–M–L)	L	L	L	L	
17. Required investment to stay competitive (H–M–L)	NA	NA	NA	NA	
18. Growth rate of total market (%)	14%	14%	14%	14%	
19. Growth rate of product's market share (%)	NA	NA	NA	NA	
20. Product's market share of total market (%)	35%	NA	NA	NA	
21. Estimated profit margin (%)	18%	NA	NA	NA	
22. Supplier power (H–M–L)	L	L	M	M	
23. Buyer power (H–M–L)	M	M	M	M	

NA = Not available or unknown.

SECTION D   **Product:**   Hard Disk Drive

Competitor: Competitor A

1. Does this firm offer complementary products?

Their offering	**Our product equivalent**
No	None

2. Do they have technological advantages over our products?

Their offering and its advantages	**Our product equivalent**
No current offering, but they are expected to catch up in one to two years. Specific products not known.	AutoDrive—leading-edge product, has very promising future.

3. Do they add value to any products above ours?

Their offering and its value added	Our product equivalent
Yes—packaging, promotion, discounts, add-ons.	Limited discounts and add-on feature capability.

4. Are they a niche company?

List niches and product offering in each	Our product equivalent
Yes—same market segments we are in.	AutoDrive.

5. Is their pricing strategy by individual product, segment, or both?

List their pricing strategy

Predatory pricing to gain market share; often deep discounts to obtain large customer accounts.

Usually based on product, but if a segment is price sensitive, price changes to that segment are

made as a whole.

6. What percent have they gone above or below the price of their product to make a sale?

Product offering and price variance	Our product equivalent
Plus or minus 23% off list price.	Plus or minus 14% off list price.

7. Do you feel this firm is cutting prices to gain market share for the long run? If yes, which products and how?

Product	Method of price cutting
Yes, hard disk drive. They are decreasing prices, since their products are behind AutoDrive in technology. Thus, the larger the market share they get by cutting prices, the more of that share they can migrate to their new product, which will be equal to or better than AutoDrive.	Cutting prices, but not sure by how much or to whom. Could be suppliers or retail markets.

8. What customer voids do their products fill that our product(s) do not?

Competitor's products	Associated customer voids
Currently none. However, we understand that their hard disk drives will be compatible with the two largest computer manufacturers while ours is aimed at small computer and compatible companies.	Customers whose products are compatible with major computer firm products; easy interface.

9. What type of distribution channels do they use?

Direct mail, direct response; wholesalers; sales reps.

10. What is the geographic coverage of their distribution system?

Nationwide. But for this product they are using a niche strategy. Strategy is to start in the

Midwest and then expand.

11. What geographic area are they targeting as their market?

Not sure, but generally the same area as ours, probably the Midwest.

12. Do you feel this is an innovative firm?

Yes, past history of firm indicates its management is very proactive, and it is a high-growth

firm.

13. Is this firm a leader or follower?

Usually a leader, but in this case they are a follower, waiting to see if our product is

successful.

14. Do customers see this firm's products as technologically superior or inferior to ours?

They are rated above average in quality and service, but slightly below our level.

15. What product applications does this firm have above or below our offerings?

Not sure, because their new product is not out yet; but as of now, current product is

technologically inferior to ours and has limited applications.

_____

16. List specific target markets/segments for each competitor product.

Product	Target market/segment
Hard disk drive.	Not sure what segment will be targeted for
	new product, but it will probably be the same
	as ours.

CHAPTER THREE

Step 2:
Product Positioning

Introduction

Many successful companies use the procedures in this chapter to determine product performance and market position. When you have completed Form 3: Product Evaluation Questionnaire and the Business Profile and Business Assessment matrices presented in this chapter, you will be able to see clearly the current status of each product and its future based on your present marketing strategy. In addition, any strategic gaps between your current and expected position will become evident. You can then determine whether you need to make changes in your current strategy or to develop a new strategic approach.

While information about each product's current position and its projected three-year position is important, the critical question is: Will you meet the objectives of your company in three years based on your *current strategies only?* If not, then you must determine the weaknesses and voids in your current product strategies and make the needed changes that will close the strategic gaps between your projected and desired outcomes. Products must be positioned effectively so that over the three-year time horizon you will be able to meet your marketing and company objectives. This process emphasizes the proactive nature of successful marketing plans.

However, knowing the position and strategic gaps of each product by itself tells only part of the story regarding that product's effect on your total line. Thus, in Chapter 4 we show you how to evaluate your entire product portfolio over the next three years, again based on your current strategy. We use two additional matrices in Chapter 4 to suggest strategies for strengthening your product portfolio.

The approach we have chosen to define product position is one among several that can be used. However, we feel that this method is one of the most valuable in generating product information for the development of strategies. As you become more familiar with the techniques of product positioning and portfolio analysis, you may decide to use more elaborate mapping approaches than the ones presented in this book. Our purpose here is to give you a sound understanding of product positioning and evaluating product portfolios for use in developing your marketing strategies.

As you work through this chapter, you will draw on the data you developed for the questionnaire in Chapter 2. In this chapter we also ask you to rate various items qualitatively for Form 3: Product Evaluation Questionnaire, but you will now assign numeric values to the questions to plot the position of your products on the Business Profile and Business Assessment matrices. The same approach is used in Chapter 4 for the Growth–Share matrices. In this method, you use qualitative data and convert it to quantitative data to determine the state of your company's products or strategic business units. *Strategic business units* (SBUs) are defined as one or more company divisions, a product line within a company, or even a single product. They generally have their own missions and objectives and may have their own marketing plans separate from other businesses within a firm.

The Sample Case at the end of the chapter presents a completed questionnaire and matrices for current and three-year projections. To understand how these planning tools are created and used in a real-world situation, carefully read through the chapter and the case.

Product Positioning—Micro View

Product positioning analysis is a critical part of environmental assessment. Through this process, product managers determine the nature, interrelationships, and impact of environmental factors on the individual product, and anticipate trends important to the product's future. This allows you to manage the product more effectively and to reduce guesswork or internal biases about the product and the marketplace.

Positioning Analysis

To accomplish this, market managers must make reasonable assumptions about demographic, economic, technological, political, and cultural changes. They should be aware of these underlying assumptions and, to the degree possible, test their reasonableness against what can be observed in the environment.

Product positioning analysis includes the development of certain matrices to determine competitive position, life cycle stage, market attractiveness, growth–share, and business strengths and weaknesses. These matrices reflect both controllable and uncontrollable variables. The best marketing strategy will help a firm make the most of variables it can control and adapt effectively to those it cannot control.

Starting the Analysis

To begin the analysis, you need the following information about each product: its competitive position, stage of the product life cycle, business strengths and weaknesses, market attractiveness, growth rate, and market share. You should be able to obtain this information from Form 2: Assessing the Competition, which you completed for each of your firm's products.

Remember, it may seem at the outset that positioning analysis is concerned only with an individual product or an SBU's position. When all the products are combined into a single company portfolio, however, you will discover a great deal about your firm; e.g., its competitive strengths, market share, problems and opportunities, and potential gaps in your strategies to reach your objectives. All strategies must work together to meet the objectives set by the overall corporate business plan.

The purpose of Form 3: Product Evaluation Questionnaire is to define key questions or attributes affecting a product and to assign a numeric weighting system to them to help lower internal bias, expand the scope of attributes affecting your product's future, and define strategic gaps.

Business Profile Matrix

The Business Profile Matrix, as shown in Figure 3.1, indicates the relationship between a product's *competitive position* and its *current life cycle stage*. To complete the Business Profile Matrix, the marketing manager must determine the current life cycle stage of the product and the stage it will be in after three years.

Data from the Product Evaluation Questionnaire will help you to determine the major weaknesses or gaps in the product's performance. The matrix suggests whether the product can be repositioned along its life cycle to maintain or increase its competitive position.

The vertical axis of the matrix—competitive position—indicates the position of the product in relation to its direct and indirect competition. The horizontal axis represents the product's current life cycle stage.

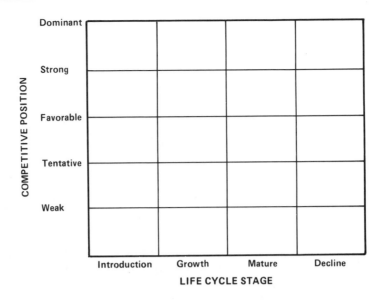

Figure 3.1   Business Profile Matrix

The information obtained from plotting this matrix can help you to determine the appropriate marketing strategy to improve a product's competitive position throughout its life cycle. The relationship between competitive position and life cycle stage of a product is critical when deciding how to allocate assets for product support or whether to keep the product in your portfolio. Say, for example, the product is in its Introduction Stage and falls in the strong competitive cell on the matrix. A successful marketing strategy may include moving the product into its Growth Stage and improving its competitive position (thus increasing revenues) by doing the following:

1. Using promotional tactics to increase buyer awareness.
2. Determining optimal distribution channels, setting appropriate pricing, and so on.

In this instance, you can see that your product is in a strong competitive position before moving into the Growth Stage where competition begins to intensify and market share is increasingly difficult to obtain.

On the other hand, suppose the data reveal that a product is in its late Growth Stage in only the "favorable" cell and is projected to fall to the "tentative" cell. Its competitive position will then decline, resulting in a lower market share.

This information is important, since in the Mature Stage of a life cycle, competition is intense and profit margins correspondingly narrow. It is much more difficult to gain an increased share of the market without considerable cost to the firm. The available market is smaller, and brand loyalty has already been established by other firms. Considerable advertising funds may be needed to convince new customers to buy or switch from their current products. In this case, the return on investment may fall to an unacceptable level, and the product will need a large cash outflow to keep its current weak market share.

In working with this matrix, you will generate the following information for each product:

1. Define where your products currently are.
2. Determine their projected position three years from now with respect to the market for all products. (In this book, we are using a three-year projection as an example.)
3. Assess whether to continue or drop any product offering or to devise corrective strategies to ensure that you meet your corporate objectives.

A completed Business Profile Matrix is provided in the sample Product Evaluation Questionnaire at the end of this chapter.

Business Assessment Matrix

The Business Assessment Matrix, shown in Figure 3.2, indicates the relationship between the *business strengths* supporting a product and the *attractiveness of the market* for product investment.

The vertical axis of the matrix—business strengths—shows the product's ability to compete in a particular industry. Business strength is usually a weighted rating of factors such as product quality, price competitiveness, relative market share, and other pertinent variables.

The horizontal axis—market attractiveness—is based on a weighted rating of factors such as sensitivity to economic conditions, market size, competitive intensity, profitability, market growth, and other relevant variables.

As shown in Figure 3.2, the matrix is divided into three sections: Growth, Selectivity, and Harvest.

The *Growth section* consists of three cells which indicate markets that are favorable or high in market attractiveness and business strengths for your company's products. An appropriate marketing strategy would be to invest for growth in those products.

The *Selectivity section* indicates markets that have medium market attractiveness and business strengths. The best strategy may be simply to maintain the product's share of this market rather than attempt to increase or reduce it.

The *Harvest section* consists of matrix cells that indicate markets with low overall market attractiveness and business strengths. A sug-

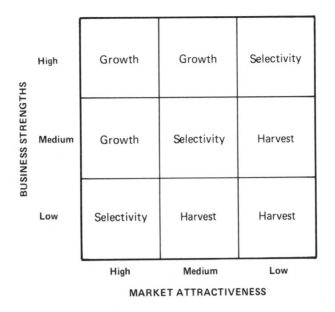

Figure 3.2 **Business Assessment Matrix**

gested strategy here may be to divest products in these markets if the products cannot be repositioned favorably. The main point is not to spend additional funds on products that produce low revenues or a loss.

The matrix, then, presents a graphic and analytic picture of a product's investment and return possibilities based on market conditions and on the company's capabilities. This method has been used successfully in many companies.

As in the Business Profile Matrix, the numeric values assigned to the questionnaire items will help you to position products on the Business Assessment Matrix. Although in our example we use only a few attributes in the composite, you can add to or delete the number of attributes. This process is a perfect application for a personal computer, which can make this matrix a dynamic planning tool.

In addition to the general strategies mentioned earlier, the Business Assessment Matrix allows marketing managers to determine which factors have the greatest or the least influence on product position. For example, the following four critical success factors for one of your products may be ranked as follows: "high" market growth, "large" market size, "low" competitive intensity, and "low" profitability.

Since three of the four critical factors are positive, at first glance the product seems to be in a strong position. But the fourth critical factor—low profitability—changes the picture. As a result, even though the product is placed in the high growth cell, you discover that

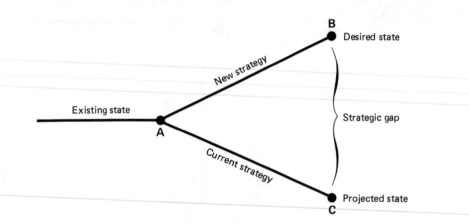

Figure 3.3 Strategic Gap Analysis

return on investment is below company objectives. For this reason, it is important to look at all of the critical factors relating to a product. Although the initial results may look positive, only one or two negative factors can alter the results considerably. In the case of our example, your firm has a high-growth product that yields little or no profit.

The next step is to determine why profit is so low. For this, go back to your original profitability analysis, conducted in the basis view, on the Competitive Assessment Questionnaire. A careful check of that analysis should help you determine the factors that are pulling down profitability and whether the problem can be corrected.

Strategic Gap Analysis

To illustrate how strategies relate to product planning, we first consider the strategic gap analysis depicted in Figure 3.3.

Point A represents the current position of a product. Point B is the desired position that the product manager would like to see the product attain within, say, three years, based on current product plans. However, the firm's current strategies and assumptions about its environment may actually place the product at point C in three years. The difference between point B and point C is known as the *strategic gap.*

If the gap is considered significant and can be reduced, the firm can then make strategic decisions to change product plans and objectives in order to close the gap, shifting the product closer to point B. If the gap is not considered significant, or if through various circumstances beyond the company's control the gap cannot be closed, then no change in strategy is called for. The company may simply allow the product to reach point C.

Let's look at a brief example of how product managers can use this process to their advantage in developing product strategies. Look over the Business Profile Matrix in Figure 3.4.

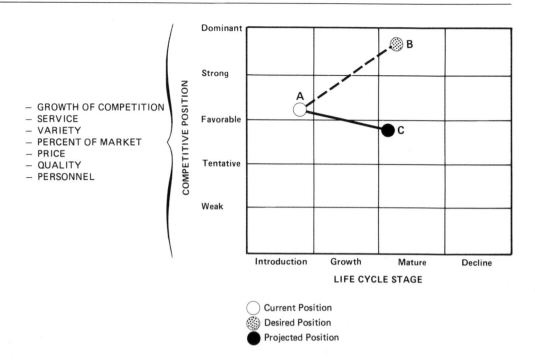

- GROWTH OF COMPETITION
- SERVICE
- VARIETY
- PERCENT OF MARKET
- PRICE
- QUALITY
- PERSONNEL

Figure 3.4 Business Profile Matrix—Sample Strategic Gap Analysis

Point A is current product position; point C is the projected position based on data from the Product Evaluation Questionnaire; and point B is where you want your product to be in three years based on today's strategies. The area on the matrix between points B and C is your strategic gap.

If you wish to close this gap to reach your desired position, first look at those attributes in the product evaluation that you considered *critical* to the success of your product. Determine which attributes are having a negative influence and whether you can control or change the attributes by changing your strategies. For example, if new legislation makes it more difficult to sell your product across the state line, can you work to modify the legislation or to have your product exempt from coverage?

If you cannot change the influence of these attributes on your product's future position, examine your contingency plans for new action. Perhaps you can offer more services with the product or develop a new pricing structure to undercut the competition. Follow these steps for those attributes that you consider *medium* and *low* in importance.

This process can assist you in three ways. First, it helps you to decide what strategic changes, if any, are necessary to close the gap. Second, it points out the strengths and weaknesses of your current strategies and objectives. Third, and most important, it serves as an early warning system to define problems and bring them to your attention now instead of a year or so later when it may be too late to make changes.

This process underscores the importance of conducting a sound environmental assessment before developing strategies and objectives for the coming year or years. The strategic gap analysis can be a valuable tool in your strategy development.

Once you have completed the Product Evaluation Questionnaire, Business Profile Matrix, and Business Assessment Matrix for each product, you will need to put all the data together in a global or macro view for strategic planning. We explain the macro view in Chapter 4, Portfolio Analysis. Although we are concerned only with the strategic level in this book, the data you develop in these chapters will also help you in your tactical planning.

The Product Evaluation Questionnaire

Many firms do not have adequate techniques to assess quantitatively all the variables that the basis view considers. Therefore, we provide Form 3: Product Evaluation Questionnaire, which will help you analyze each product's environment. It combines both internal and external factors and provides a rating system which is then used to plot a product's current and projected position on the Business Profile and Business Assessment matrices.

You can modify the Product Evaluation Questionnaire to fit your company's needs, deleting variables that are irrelevant to your situation and adding those that are important. The questionnaire enables you to translate qualitative statements into measurable terms and results. The objective of the questionnaire is twofold: first, to determine whether your products are moving toward your company goals; and second, to help you obtain a clear picture of individual product positions and potential problems and opportunities. If the products are not moving toward the stated objectives and strategies (desired outcomes), then a strategic gap exists and you need to determine how to close the gap.

Defining the Terms

Terms used in the questionnaire are defined here. They are numbered to correspond to the sections in the questionnaire. Because these terms may have different meanings to different individuals, clarity is essential.

Section I.   Competitive Position

1. *Price:* Extent to which the product enjoys a price advantage over the competition. In general, the product with a lower price has the advantage. If the item is clearly differentiated from the competition, however,

the product manager has more latitude in setting the price, depending on the marketing strategy chosen.

2. *Quality:* Product's quality relative to competing products. Quality is the rated ability of the product to fulfill its function. It is an overall measure of the product's features such as durability, reliability, precision, ease of operation, and maintenance and repair.

3. *Percent of market:* Product's sales expressed as a percent of total market sales. Total market sales consist of the product's sales plus the sales of all substitute products.

4. *Variety:* Number of different items in a product line or the number of different features associated with a product. Variety enables a product or product line to attract customers who have different preferences and needs.

5. *Sales personnel:* Comparison of the firm's sales force with its competitors' in terms of product knowledge, knowledge of customers and competitors, sales skills, and efficiency.

6. *Breadth of product application:* Number of different uses for the product relative to competing products.

7. *Relation to other product lines:* How closely related the firm's product is to their other products in terms of its end use. This can lead to a price cross-elastic effect.

8. *Service:* Extent to which the company offers better service for its products than do competitors. Service includes the types and levels of delivery, installation, and maintenance provided by the firm and its competitors.

    Evaluating service requires an understanding of the importance of such elements to customers and a knowledge of what determines customer choice. It is possible for a service element to be important and yet not be a determinant of customer choice if all the firms in the market provide the same service level.

9. *Growth of competition:* Entry of new competitors and products into the market and extent to which the market share of competitive products has increased.

10. *Assortment:* Does your firm have a greater assortment of products than the major competitors offer?

11. *Supplier power:* Extent to which your supplier can exert pressure over necessary resources and also enter your market place.

12. *Substitution threat:* Potential of competitors to offer substitute products that can take market share and sales away from you.

Section II.   Market Attractiveness

1. *Required investment:* Financial resources which must be invested in all functional areas to compete effectively.

2. *New competitive threat:* Actual or potential loss of business to new competitors. The threat of new competition is dependent on the existence of entry barriers and on the expected reaction of existing competitors.

3. *Risk:* Measure of the level of uncertainty. As the rate of environmental change accelerates, the level of uncertainty increases; for example, new products and new competitors add to environmental uncertainty.

4. *Product life expectancy:* Expected life of a product in the marketplace.

5. *Price elasticity to market demand:* Sensitivity of demand for a product when price is increased or decreased.

6. *Market growth in dollars:* Measure in dollars of the expected growth level of market demand. Market demand is the total of all sales of a product and its substitutes in a defined geographic area within a defined time period. It is affected by industry marketing efforts and the environment in general. Also, units can be used and converted to dollars.

7. *Cyclicality:* Extent to which the pattern of demand for the product is marked by seasonal or volatile fluctuations. If the fluctuations of demand are not synchronized with the pattern of supply, cyclicality can be a serious problem.

8. *Market size in dollars:* Total dollar value of the market.

9. *Profitability—actual or estimated:* Actual or estimated profit by product after expenses and taxes.

10. *Segmentation:* Division of a market into distinct subsets of customers who merit separate marketing programming and effort.

11. *Seasonality:* Certain times during the year when demand changes and affects growth.

12. *Regulatory climate:* Extent to which laws and regulations affect strategic choices.

13. *Customer negotiating/buyer power:* Power of customers to negotiate changes in price or other factors when purchasing a product or service.

14. *Return on investment (compared to company yardstick):* Estimated return on investment that the product will generate (as a total or by SBU or product).

15. *Distribution:* Available distribution systems and their effectiveness in channeling the product to the target market.

16. *Lateral effect on sales of companion products:* Amount of cross-elasticity that exists among products in your firm.

17. *Transactions generated:* Number of original purchases and the frequency of repeat purchases.

Section III. Business Strengths

1. *Geographic coverage:* Geographic constraints on product sales. Geographic constraints are desirable if market potentials and cost vary according to location and if the product is available in markets the firm can best serve.

2. *Distribution (current system):* Evaluation of the distribution system relative to competition on the basis of its potential for creating sales and generating costs.

3. *Product servicing:* See *Service.*

4. *Change in relative market share—three-year trend:* Change in relative market share over a three-year period (the current year and the two preceding years).

5. *Selling power:* Recognizing customer problems (needs) and providing solutions.

6. *Price competitiveness:* See *Price.*

7. *Breadth of product line:* Spectrum of products offered—a complete line or only a specific part of a complete product line.
8. *New products:* Extent to which new products or variations of present products enter your business and stimulate customers to purchase.
9. *Product differentiation:* Existence of distinctly different features, quality, style, or image that are important to the market and give products a competitive advantage.
10. *Relative market share:* Product's sales expressed as a percentage of the leading competitor's sales. A change in relative market share may be due to general environmental conditions, for example, substitute products and technology changes. Although external forces affect all competing products, they often do not affect them all equally. That is why relative market share is important. Measuring a product's performance against that of its competitors removes the influence of the general environment.
11. *Source structure:* Availability of appropriate sources to produce and market products.
12. *Product quality:* See *Quality*.
13. *Compatibility:*
    A. To what extent do your systems satisfy the needs of your product line?
    B. What relationship does this product have to other lines of business within your product group?
    C. Does the strategic direction of the product support the company's overall strategy?
14. *Drawing power:* Extent to which the firm's promotion, reputation, and brand identification can draw potential customers.

Instructions for Completing the Questionnaire

Because conditions for each company differ, you may need to adapt the Product Evaluation Questionnaire for your particular firm. Follow these steps:

1. Go through the questionnaire and decide which questions you want to use. Add or delete questions to make the questionnaire more relevant to your company.

2. Decide which questions are *critical* to your product's success, which are of *medium* importance, and which are of *low* importance. Mark the questions with a C, M, or L. These are known as critical success factors.

3. Assign a point spread to each question based on whether it is critical, medium, or low in importance. We suggest the following scale (1 is least important; 10, 7, and 4 are most important):
    Critical   1–10
    Medium   1–7
    Low   1–4

As a C, M, or L rank is assigned to a question, fill in the appropriate range of values in the *Points Assigned* column on the questionnaire. (See the completed questionnaire for the Sample Case.)

Keep in mind that on this questionnaire high values are not always good, and low values are not always bad. It all depends on the question and its importance or lack of importance to your firm. For example, if price competitiveness is a critical question for your firm's products, you would assign a value of 1 to 10 to your answers for all questions that relate to price. If any item in that category receives a 1 or 2, you would know that you are vulnerable to competition in terms of your pricing structure. A low score would be a negative indicator.

On the other hand, regulatory climate may be only of moderate concern. You would assign a value of 1 to 7 for your answers to all questions in that category. In this case, a low score would be a positive sign. Any item that receives a high score—say, 6 or 7—would indicate a potential problem for that product from the regulatory area. Perhaps the Federal Trade Commission (FTC) is considering legislation that would make it more difficult for you to sell your product in another state.

4. Fill out your adjusted questionnaire and total the values for each of the three sections: Competitive Position, Market Attractiveness, and Business Strengths. These totals will be used as plot points to map your products on the matrices provided at the end of the questionnaire.

5. To determine the point values along the *horizontal* and *vertical* axes on the Business Assessment Matrix and along the *vertical* axis on the Business Profile Matrix (the life cycle stage can be provided by the product manager), follow these steps.

- Add up the highest values assigned to the questions in the Points Assigned column for each section of the questionnaire. (The highest values in the sample questionnaire are starred.)

- Divide these totals by the number of cells along the vertical axis in each matrix. The same procedures apply to the horizontal axis in the Business Assessment Matrix. This will give you the incremental point value for each cell along each axis.

For instance, say the sum of the highest values assigned to the questions in the Competitive Position section equals 75 points. The Business Profile Matrix has five cells along the vertical axis. Therefore: 75/5 = 15. The points along the vertical axis would be set as shown in the sample matrix that follows.

If the totals of the highest points assigned are not equal for the axes on both matrices, you may want to index the totals to a base of 100. Indexing will not affect positioning of the products.

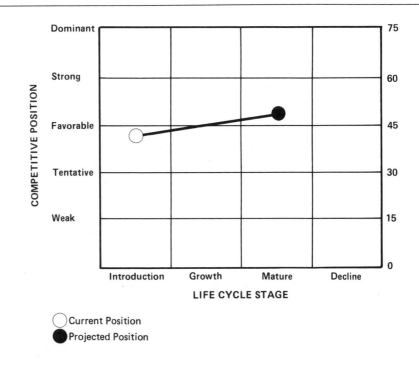

Current Position
Projected Position

Sample Business Profile Matrix

6. Add the total points under the current year and projected year columns for each section in the questionnaire. (For the sample questionnaire, current year is 1993; projected year is 1996.) These totals will enable you to plot current and projected positions for your products on the two matrices.

7. Plot your product's current and projected positions on the Business Profile and Business Assessment matrices. Suppose, for example, your product is in the Introductory Stage and has a Competitive Position total points of 44 for the current year. In three years you project that your product will be in the Mature Stage with a Competitive Position total points of 50. These positions are plotted on the Sample Business Profile Matrix.

8. Look over the current and projected product positions and write down any conclusions you may draw regarding product positions and any needed adjustments to current strategies.

9. Fill out a Product Evaluation Questionnaire for each of your company's products.

The results of the questionnaire, although not 100 percent precise, will give you a sound starting point from which to begin quantifying the qualitative data you have developed. This is particularly true for those items where little or no quantitative information is available.

The data you generate in filling out the questionnaire will be used to complete the Portfolio Business Profile, Portfolio Business Assessment, and Growth–Share matrices presented in Chapter 4. Although many matrices have been developed to help the marketing strategist in positioning analysis we suggest these particular three for an important reason. They not only provide data for strategic planning from several perspectives but also act as a check-and-balance system on the results you gain from your analysis. A problem or opportunity that shows up on the Business Profile should also appear as a similar problem or opportunity on the Business Assessment and Growth–Share matrices.

Before filling out the Product Evaluation Questionnaire, look over the completed questionnaire in the Sample Case at the end of this chapter. This will give you a better idea of the type of information the questionnaire is designed to provide. After you have finished the product evaluations, the results will guide you in formulating strategies to reposition your product from its current to its desired projected position and close any strategic gaps.

Summary

- Product positioning analysis helps managers to determine the nature, interrelationships, and impact of environmental factors on the individual product and to anticipate trends important to the product's future.

- The process allows companies to manage their products more effectively and to reduce guesswork or internal biases about the product and marketplace.

- Marketing managers must make reasonable assumptions about demographic, economic, technological, political, and cultural changes. They should test their assumptions against what can be observed in the environment.

- Product positioning analysis includes the development of certain matrices to determine competitive position, life cycle stage, market attractiveness, growth–share, and business strengths and weaknesses. The matrices reflect both controllable and uncontrollable variables.

- The Business Profile Matrix indicates the relationship between a product's competitive position and its current life cycle stage. Information obtained from plotting this matrix can help you to determine the appropriate marketing strategy to improve a product's competitive position throughout its life cycle.

- The Business Assessment Matrix indicates the relationship between the business strengths supporting a product and the attractiveness of the market for product investment. The matrix is divided into three sections: growth, selectivity, and harvest. The matrix represents a graphic and analytic picture of a product's investment and return possibilities that is based on market conditions and on the company's capabilities.

- Strategic gap analysis shows you the difference between your product's desired position and projected position. The process can help you to (1) decide what changes in strategy, if any, are necessary to close the gap, (2) detect strengths and weaknesses in your current strategies and objectives, and (3) identify problems early while there is still time to make changes.

Sample Case
"How Many of These Forms Are There?"

At the end of three weeks, Greg Haines received the results of his staff's efforts to fill in the data gaps revealed by the competitive assessment questionnaire. Although the staff were able to fill in some of the information, they still had data missing.

"What's the next step?" one of his marketing team members asked.

"We need to do a comprehensive product evaluation. I've developed a Product Evaluation Questionnaire that I want to use. It will give us more quantitative data but may still rely on managers' gut feelings for the answers to some of the questions."

The staff member looked dubious. "How can you be sure that the 'gut feeling' data has any validity to it?"

"I'll have the managers present their completed forms to me in person so I can ask questions about their answers. You'd be surprised how that improves the data I get."

Haines and the three partners called a product management meeting to explain the Product Evaluation Questionnaire. Haines first expressed his appreciation for the managers' cooperation so far, in particular emphasizing the honesty of the answers he had received.

"Now we need to gather information on each product and analyze both its current position and projected three-year position based on today's strategies.

"In the case of AutoDrive, for example, we can map its current and projected position based on data developed by market research and forecasting groups. This could include a policy to migrate current customers to the new hard disk and expand market share by finding new users nationwide.

"We can then put together a portfolio view of all the products and determine whether we like the direction they're going. If not, we'll need to develop new strategies and objectives to improve their projected positions."

One of the managers raised her hand. "Does this mean we have to fill out another form? How many of these things are there?"

Price interjected strongly, "This planning process is a high priority for the company. However many forms there are, that's how many everyone will fill out."

Haines heard the subdued murmuring that could mean rebellion if he didn't change the tone of the meeting. "I understand your feelings. No one I've ever worked with wanted to fill out these questionnaires, but they always appreciated what they learned from them. It may be a chore to do these forms, but I can guarantee that you'll get something out of it for yourselves."

Haines handed out copies of the Product Evaluation Questionnaire and explained the ranking and point systems. The marketing department had already assigned preliminary point values to the critical, medium, and low rankings; but the product managers could change the point values at their discretion. It would be up to individual product managers to assign the C, M, or L rank to each question and to use the point values associated with each rank.

"You'll have to make some assumptions in answering certain questions, but our marketing group can help you. If some assumptions have a wide variance—for instance, the growth rate of the GNP over the next three years—we'll calculate a base line that everyone can use. Let's say the growth rate will be 3.9 percent over the next three years. You'll use that figure in answering all questions that involve GNP projections.

"Some of these answers will be based on your judgment as much as on objective facts or figures. Use the comments' section to explain and support your answers. Don't worry about having to explain in any great detail. Remember, this is not a test of your knowledge, but part of a data-gathering process that is fundamental to any good plan.

"Turn in the completed forms to me personally so we'll have a chance to discuss your answers. We have a tight schedule to keep, and I'd like the questionnaire returned one week from tomorrow."

The managers agreed they would complete the form in a week's time. Haines was particularly interested in which items the product managers would consider of critical, medium, or low importance. To make sure none of them exaggerated or understated their responses, he would compare their answers with the market share data, sales figures, and other information his staff had developed independently. The managers, in turn, would be gaining valuable experience in data gathering and in analyzing their products from a marketing perspective. Haines felt confident this would make them feel more invested in the planning process, which would be a valuable asset when it came time to implement the final plan.

Within one week, Haines received the questionnaires from every manager, complete with comments, rankings, and mapping. He was pleased with the thoroughness of the responses, particularly for Auto-Drive. (The completed Product Evaluation Questionnaire for Auto-Drive can be found after the matrices at the end of this case.)

Haines analyzed the results for each product. Because AutoDrive has a five-year life span in a high-growth, fast-paced industry, he was not surprised to find that in three years AutoDrive would move to the early Mature Stage. With a longer projected life span, the downward trend would have indicated a problem. To be sure the projections are correct, Haines would need to determine whether current strategies for AutoDrive are still applicable after the portfolio analysis is completed. The next step would be to see how the entire product portfolio looked before developing strategic objectives and selecting marketing strategies.

Business Profile Matrix* (Form 3)

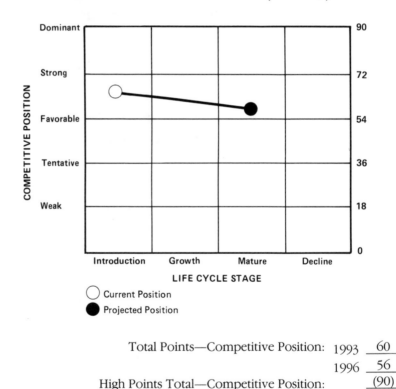

Total Points—Competitive Position: 1993 __60__

1996 __56__

High Points Total—Competitive Position: __(90)__

90/5 = 18 points per matrix cell

*Source: Product Evaluation Questionnaire.

Conclusions Drawn from Business Profile Matrix (Overview)

1. AutoDrive is in the high part of the strong cell in its Introductory Stage but will drop slightly in its Mature Stage in a very competitive market. This product is in a strong position now and in the near future.

2. AutoDrive should gain significant market share and realize a positive profit margin. Funds should be allocated now to capture large market share with possible price flexibility and taper the funds off as the product reaches its Mature Stage.

3. No major void areas exist. Those that do exist and that will allow the product to fall in competitive position are largely out of management's control, unless profit margins are also allowed to drop.

4. The marketing manager should determine specific plans to migrate current customers of the old product to AutoDrive.

5. No strategic gaps exist; product is following proper course.

Business Assessment Matrix*   (Form 3)

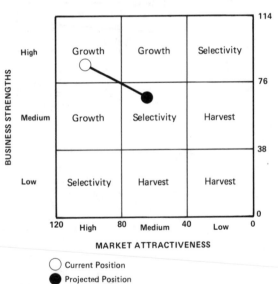

Total Points—Market Attractiveness: 1993 __88__ 1996 __61__
Total Points—Business Strengths: 1993 __102__ 1996 __73__
High Points Total—Market Attractiveness: __(120)__
  120/3 = 40 points per matrix cell
High Points Total—Business Strengths: __(114)__
  114/3 = 38 points per matrix cell

---

*Source: Product Evaluation Questionaire.

Conclusions Drawn from Business Assessment Matrix (Overview)

1. AutoDrive has very high business strengths and no major voids.

2. Market is large and very attractive to investment; market attractiveness is high, and the required business strengths exist to ensure a successful product. No strategic gaps currently occur.

3. In three years AutoDrive will decline in business strength and market attractiveness because of the great number of competitors and because the product will enter its Mature Stage. Prices and profit margins will also decrease due to highly competitive market.

4. The firm should invest only enough in AutoDrive to maintain market share once it reaches its Mature Stage. A new substitute prototype product will be out in four years to fill AutoDrive's technological voids and will become a potential market leader.

5. Timing to phase out AutoDrive and to migrate its customers to a new substitute product will be crucial in four years to maintain or increase market share for the firm as a whole.

Form 3   Product Evaluation Questionnaire

Product: __AutoDrive__   Date: _____

I. Competitive Position   Critical Success Factors Ranking (C, M, L)

Points Assigned: Critical __(1–10)__   Medium __(1–7)__   Low __(1–4)__

1. __M__ Price
   To what extent does our firm have price advantage over major competitors?

	Current 1993	Projected 1996	Points Assigned
Low		2	(2)
Moderate	4		(4)
High			(7)*

Comments
With few competitors and economies of scale, we can change price levels to increase market share when needed. In three years, many competitors will be in the market with a similar or technologically superior product. Product and market will be in early Mature Stage when competitive pricing will force profit margins down. Weaker competitors will be weeded out.

_____

*High points used to calculate High Points Total for each section.

2. __M__ Quality

To what extent does our firm have better product quality than our major competitors?

	Current 1993	Projected 1996	Points Assigned
Low			(1)
Same			(3)
Somewhat higher		5	(5)
Much higher	7		(7)*

Comments

Market research indicates that consumers see our products as higher in quality than competitors', but this will change slightly as competitors increase their quality standards to our level.

3. __C__ Percent of market

	Current 1993	Projected 1996	Points Assigned
Low			(3)
Medium		7	(7)
High	10		(10)*

Comments

Product is projected to have 12 percent of the small market by year end. In three years, market size will greatly expand; initial projections are that we will have 36 percent of that market. However, this is likely to be 28 percent due to increase in foreign competition and rapid changes in technology.

4. __M__ Variety

To what extent does our firm have a broader assortment associated with this product than do our major competitors?

	Current 1993	Projected 1996	Points Assigned
Less			(1)
Equal		3	(3)
Moderate	5		(5)
High			(7)*

Comments

Product has limited valued-added features now; more will be added later. Therefore, product line is not complete for all market segments. In three years, competition will offer same features.

5. <u>M</u> Sales personnel

How does our firm's sales staff compare with our major competitors'?

	Current 1993	Projected 1996	Points Assigned
Low			(2)
Equal	4		(4)
Better		7	(7)*

Comments

Firm has extensive training and excellent compensation but needs two-month learning curve for full national coverage and consideration of overseas coverage.

6. <u>M</u> Breadth of product application

	Current 1993	Projected 1996	Points Assigned
Narrow			(2)
Average	4		(4)
Broad		7	(7)*

Comments

Product was placed on market early to beat competition, but not all applications were available. In one year, breadth will be great enough to meet the needs of target market segments.

7. <u>L</u> Relation to other company product lines

	Current 1993	Projected 1996	Points Assigned
Little/no compatibility			(0)
Moderate		1	(1)
Good	2		(2)
Excellent			(3)*

Comments

Product is in same product line as other offerings but is technologically superior. Several current products can be used with this product, but in three years its technology will decline. Other company products will change to new technology and will not be as adaptive to this product.

8. __M__ Service

How does our firm's service compare with major competitors'?

	Current 1993	Projected 1996	Points Assigned
Less			(1)
Same	3		(3)
Moderately better			(5)
High		7	(7)*

Comments

High service is a major corporate goal. Firm has good training, high compensation, and incentives; but two-month learning curve is still needed before we are better than competitors. Firm will have national coverage possibly in one year.

9. __C__ Growth of competition

	Current 1993	Projected 1996	Points Assigned
Low	10		(10)*
Moderate			(6)
High		3	(3)

Comments

Product is in Introductory Stage; it has few competitors, but number will rise substantially as high demand and large profit margins draw them into market. Product also matures in about three years, and at that point, market will be saturated.

10. __M__ Assortment

To what extent does our firm have broader assortment than our major competitor has?

	Current 1993	Projected 1996	Points Assigned
Low			(2)
Same		4	(4)

	Current 1993	Projected 1996	Points Assigned
Moderately higher	6		(6)
High			(8)*

Comments
Currently we have technological edge and complementary products. In three years competition will offer same lines of products.

11. __C__ Supplier power
   To what extent can suppliers exert pressure over necessary resources and possibly enter our market?

	Current 1993	Projected 1996	Points Assigned
Low	3	3	(3)
Medium			(7)
High			(10)*

Comments
Suppliers are many and procurement of resources is readily available. Suppliers are not currently interested in entering this highly competitive market.

12. __M__ Substitution threat
   To what extent can competitors produce and supply equal or better substitute products over our offering?

	Current 1993	Projected 1996	Points Assigned
Low	2		(2)
Medium			(4)
High		7	(7)*

Comments
We have few competitors now, but product is fairly easy to copy in near future. This will cause many substitute products to be developed by competitors.

Total Points—Competitive Position:	60	56	

Competitive Position—High Points Total: (90)

II. Market Attractiveness   Critical Success Factors Ranking (C, M, L)

Points Assigned: Critical ___(1–10)___   Medium ___(1–7)___   Low ___(1–4)___

1. __M__ Required investment

	Current 1993	Projected 1996	Points Assigned
Low			(7)*
Medium	4		(4)
High		2	(2)

Comments
Capacity expansion is needed now, but firm has estimated peak demand in three years and that there will be no new capacity or other major capital expenditures required for near term future growth. Marketing mix expenditures are expected to increase substantially to stay competitive in three years.

2. __M__ New competitive threat

	Current 1993	Projected 1996	Points Assigned
Low	7		(7)*
Moderate			(4)
High		2	(2)

Comments
There are few competitors today; but since demand and profits are currently high, this market will attract many competitors.

3. __M__ Risk
New products, new competitors, new fashions

	Current 1993	Projected 1996	Points Assigned
Low	7		(7)*
Moderate		4	(4)
High			(2)

Comments
High demand estimates and few competitors equal lower risk. In three years, many competitors and lower profits will increase risk of loss of market share and future profits.

4. <u>L</u> Product life expectancy

	Current 1993	Projected 1996	Points Assigned
Low	4	4	(4)*
Moderate			(2)
High			(0)

Comments
Product is leader in technology now but in three years will mature. New, technologically superior products will start to appear. Thus, product has short life cycle of five years.

5. <u>L</u> Price elasticity to market demand

	Current 1993	Projected 1996	Points Assigned
Demand greatly reduced as price rises			(1)
Demand moderately reduced			(2)
Demand slightly reduced	3	3	(3)
Demand not affected			(4)*

Comments
Price elasticity for this product is low.

6. <u>C</u> Market growth—dollars

	Current 1993	Projected 1996	Points Assigned
Declining			(0)
Stationary		3	(3)
Moderate			(7)
Good	10		(10)*

Comments
Fast growth now is due to high demand and few competitors. In two years, many competitors will be in the market. Market will begin saturation, and new, technologically superior products will appear.

7. _L_ Cyclicality (of demand)

	Current 1993	Projected 1996	Points Assigned
Fluctuating		1	(1)
Moderate	2		(2)
Stable			(4)*

Comments
Cyclicality is only moderate now. In three years, economic conditions may cause cycles to appear and affect demand patterns of customers.

8. _C_ Market size—$ volume (000)

	Current 1993	Projected 1996	Points Assigned
To $300	2		(2)
$301 to $600			(4)
$601 to $1,000		7	(7)
More than $1,000			(10)*

Comments
Market size is estimated to increase substantially over next three years based on market and demand research.

9. _C_ Profitability—actual or estimated

	Current 1993	Projected 1996	Points Assigned
Red			(0)
0–5%		4	(4)
6–11%			(7)
12% and above	10		(10)*

Comments
Profit margins are high now due to economies of scale and few competitors. When product reaches Mature Stage, all firms will have equal economies. To increase market share, our firm and many competitors will lower price and thus, profit margins.

10. __M__ Segmentation
How easily can the market for this product be segmented?

	Current 1993	Projected 1996	Points Assigned
Difficult			(2)
Moderately easy	4	4	(4)
Easy			(7)*

Comments

Market is moderately easy to segment into customer groupings. This is not expected to change within the next three years.

11. __L__ Seasonality

	Current 1993	Projected 1996	Points Assigned
Yes			(1)
Partial	2	2	(2)
None			(4)*

Comments

Certain times of year affect orders to a small extent, but overall, no definite seasonality exists that significantly affects demand for product lines.

12. __L__ Regulatory climate
How much are quality, specifications, price, environmental concerns affected?

	Current 1993	Projected 1996	Points Assigned
Little or none	4	4	(4)*
Moderately regulated			(2)
Highly regulated			(1)

Comments

There is no government regulation in this competitive market because of the great number of competitors.

13. __M__ Customer negotiating/buyer power

	Current 1993	Projected 1996	Points Assigned
Low			(2)
Moderate	4		(4)
High		7	(7)*

Comments
Currently, only large customers have negotiating power. As competitors increase, all customers will have equal bargaining power. We will need to adjust prices to stay competitive and maintain market share.

14. __C__ Return on investment (compared to company yardstick)

	Current 1993	Projected 1996	Points Assigned
Low		3	(3)
Moderate			(7)
High	10		(10)*

Comments
High return now is due to low number of competitors, but in three years competition will increase and reduce profit margin.

15. __C__ Distribution

	Current 1993	Projected 1996	Points Assigned
Poor			(2)
Average		4	(4)
Good	7		(7)
Excellent			(10)*

Comments
Compared with our competitors, our product will be national and offered through a cost efficient distribution system. In three years competitors' products will be similar to ours with equally good distribution coverage.

16. __M__ Lateral effect on sales of companion products

	Current 1993	Projected 1996	Points Assigned
Low		3	(3)
Medium	4		(4)
High			(7)*

Comments

Product now has effect of customers choosing it over others. As entire line changes to technologically superior products, this effect will be minimal.

17. __M__ Transactions generated

	Current 1993	Projected 1996	Points Assigned
1 purchase every 3 years or longer			(2)
1 purchase every 2 to 3 years or longer	4	4	(4)
1 purchase every 1 to 2 years			(6)
1 purchase every 6 months to 1 year			(8)*

Comments

Buyers purchase this product only as needed and do not regard it as a high repeat purchase unless product breaks, is destroyed, or stolen.

Total Points—Market Attractiveness: __88__ __61__

Market Attractiveness—High Points Total: __(120)__

III. Business Strengths   Critical Success Factors Ranking (C, M, L)

Points Assigned: Critical __(1–10)__   Medium __(1–7)__   Low __(1–4)__

1. __M__ Geographic coverage

	Current 1993	Projected 1996	Points Assigned
Limited	1		(1)
Moderate			(3)
Large		5	(5)*

Comments

Firm has national coverage available by distribution system and sales offices, but production capacity constraints limit national coverage for at least one year.

2. __C__ Distribution (current system)

	Current 1993	Projected 1996	Points Assigned
Poor			(0)
Average		4	(4)
Good	7		(7)
Excellent			(10)*

Comments

Compared with competitors, our product distribution system is national and cost efficient. In three years, competitors' products will be similar to ours with equally good distribution coverage.

3. __M__ Product servicing

How does our firm's repair/servicing compare with that of competitors?

	Current 1993	Projected 1996	Points Assigned
Low			(2)
Equal	5		(5)
Better		7	(7)*

Comments

High service is a major corporate goal. Firm has good service, training, high compensation and incentives, etc., but two-month learning curve is still needed. Firm will have national and possibly overseas coverage in one year.

4. __C__ Change in market share—three-year historical trend. If less than three years, use available data.

	Current 1993	Projected 1996	Points Assigned
Declining			(0)
Stationary		4	(4)

	Current 1993	Projected 1996	Points Assigned
Moderately increasing	_____	_____	__(7)__
Greatly increasing	__10__	_____	__(10)*__

Comments

Market share is greatly increasing. As product enters Mature Stage, demand declines, market becomes saturated, and many competitors have entered the field. Market share growth will remain stationary with changes occurring only with major price reductions in Mature Stage.

5. __M__ Selling power

	Current 1993	Projected 1996	Points Assigned
Low	_____	_____	__(2)__
Below average	_____	_____	__(4)__
Average	__6__	_____	__(6)__
High	_____	__8__	__(8)*__

Comments

With few competitors and economies of scale, we can change price levels to increase market share when needed. In three years, many competitors will be in the market with similar or superior product. Product/market will be in early Mature Stage when competitive pricing will force profit margins down.

6. __C__ Price competitiveness

	Current 1993	Projected 1996	Points Assigned
Low	_____	_____	__(3)__
Moderate	_____	__6__	__(6)__
High	__10__	_____	__(10)*__

Comments

We can meet all prices of competitors now because of cost structure. In future, their cost structure will resemble ours. We want to keep the minimum ROI as stated in our objectives, so we will not compete as vigorously as our competitors. As a result, we want large market share now but also want to be in a position to move customers to our new substitute product in four years. This indicates a future market decline.

7. __M__ Breadth of product line

	Current 1993	Projected 1996	Points Assigned
Narrow			(2)
Average			(5)
Broad	7	7	(7)*

Comments

We carry a complete product line and plan to continue this strategy to fill all of our defined target markets.

8. __L__ New products

To what extent do new products or variations of present products enter our business and stimulate customers to purchase?

	Current 1993	Projected 1996	Points Assigned
Seldom			(1)
Occasionally		3	(3)
Average	5		(5)*

Comments

There are many new products now, but market will become saturated; newer products may have to be aimed at certain niches.

9. __M__ Product differentiation

	Current 1993	Projected 1996	Points Assigned
Difficult		2	(2)
Moderately difficult			(4)
Easy	7		(7)*

Comments

Competitors' current products are inferior in performance and features. Therefore, we can easily differentiate our products as technologically superior. In three years, all products will have the same features and level of technology, and differentiation via advertising will cost more than the market share gained will justify.

10. __C__ Market share

	Current 1993	Projected 1996	Points Assigned
0–7%	_____	_____	__(1)__
8–14%	_____	_____	__(3)__
15–21%	_____	6	__(6)__
22–30%	_____	_____	__(8)__
31% and over	10	_____	__(10)*__

Comments

We know current relative market share, and our forecast served as the basis for our answer about market share in three years.

11. __M__ Source structure

	Current 1993	Projected 1996	Points Assigned
Poor	_____	_____	__(1)__
Fair	_____	_____	__(3)__
Average	_____	_____	__(5)__
Good	7	7	__(7)*__

Comments

Source structure is good and is expected to continue.

12. __M__ Product quality

To what extent does our firm have better quality than our competitors?

	Current 1993	Projected 1996	Points Assigned
Lower	_____	_____	__(1)__
Same	_____	_____	__(3)__
Moderately higher	_____	5	__(5)__
Higher	7	_____	__(7)*__

Comments
Market research indicates that consumers see our products as higher in quality than competitors', but this will change slightly as competition increases.

13. __M__ Compatibility
   A. To what extent do our systems satisfy needs of our product line?

	Current 1993	Projected 1996	Points Assigned
Little or no compatibility			(1)
Moderate		2	(2)
Good	3		(3)
Excellent			(4)*

Comments
High technology of product today enhances current product line, but in three years competitor product will equal or exceed this product's technology, and compatibility may change.

   __L__ B. Relation to other lines within our product group

	Current 1993	Projected 1996	Points Assigned
Little or no compatibility			(1)
Moderate		2	(2)
Good	3		(3)*

Comments
As of today, the relation to other lines is very good because current products are compatible technologically with product, but in three years many products will not be compatible because of technological changes.

   __C__ C. Corporate strategy and other product lines

	Current 1993	Projected 1996	Points Assigned
Little or no compatibility			(2)
Moderate		4	(4)

			Points
			Assigned
Good	_____	_____	(7)
Excellent	10	_____	(10)*

Comments

Management wants frontier products with high return and large market share to complement firm's growth strategy. This need declines as product enters Mature Stage with large market share but reduced profit margins. Introduction of new products to replace obsolete products will continue as product enters Decline Stage.

14. __L__ Drawing power

	Current 1993	Projected 1996	Points Assigned
Poor	_____	_____	(0)
Below average	_____	1	(1)
Average	_____	_____	(2)
High	4	_____	(4)*

Comments

Since we have new technology today, we draw new customers from competitors and other areas. In three years all products will be similar as competition increases. Brand awareness will aid us in early stages of product sales.

Total Points—Business Strengths: ___102___ ___73___

Business Strengths—High Points Total: ___(114)___

CHAPTER FOUR

Step 3:
Portfolio Analysis

Introduction

Up to this point, we have talked about single products in the environmental analysis. Portfolio analysis looks at the total company picture. The firm must have a systematic approach to understand how all products fit together and how the product mix affects overall asset allocation for each product and strategy. This in turn will affect individual product plans, since each individual plan is a part of the total marketing plan to reach company objectives.

Portfolio analysis provides an overall picture of the current and projected position of your company's product portfolio as dictated by your current strategy. In this chapter we use Portfolio Business Profile and Portfolio Business Assessment matrices, Growth–Share Matrix, and Product Dynamic Matrix to map out current and projected positions. The information gathered from this analysis will help you to select strategies to reposition products and achieve your company's growth and market share goals.

Portfolio Analysis—Macro View

A company with several divisions and products has an important advantage over undiversified firms. It can channel its resources into the most productive units rather than allocate all funds to only one product line and hope for the best. Successful companies often conduct integrated strategic planning at the corporate or division level to match resources with product potential and to establish when and how the transfers of resources should take place.

For example, a diversified conglomerate may choose to slow

down the growth of its electronic games division so that it can divert the cash to expand its business software division. Such integrated planning may deliberately downplay one division's activities in favor of increasing total corporate performance.

The product portfolio approach, which we are using in this chapter, differs in an important way from other integrative planning techniques. In the product portfolio method, strategic roles are assigned to each product on the basis of the product's market growth rate and market share relative to competition.

We then integrate these individual roles into a corporate strategy for the whole portfolio of products, taking into account the product portfolios of significant competitors. This analysis will show differences unique to each product in terms of growth potential, relative market share and, hence, cash flow potential. In turn, these differences will determine which products (1) represent investment opportunities, (2) should supply investment funds, or (3) may be candidates for elimination from the portfolio.

The objective of this analysis is to get the best overall performance from the portfolio, while at the same time keeping cash flow in balance.

If a company's products are in different industries—for example, book publishing and foodservice—the firm cannot compare the product lines directly. The managers will have to develop separate portfolios for each industry product line.

Portfolio Business Profile and Business Assessment Matrices

Figures 4.1 and 4.2 show the Portfolio Business Profile and Portfolio Business Assessment matrices used to plot six products of a firm whose products' average life span is less than five years. This is a very dynamic portfolio, constantly changing through innovation and the introduction of new products. The matrices show the movement of the products over time—that is, where they will be in three years. The matrices are used to identify strategic gaps and to balance the portfolio in terms of cash flow, market share, and contribution margin.

Notice the similarities between the two matrices regarding product movements. This demonstrates the check-and-balance system mentioned in Chapter 3. The results you obtain on one matrix should be reflected in the results obtained on the other matrices.

There are several ways to display relevant information about your firm's portfolio and make the complexities of the analysis somewhat more manageable. To do so, we move from the Portfolio Business Profile and Portfolio Business Assessment matrices to the Growth–Share Matrix. Keep in mind, however, that the profile and assessment matrices are an important part of your portfolio analysis.

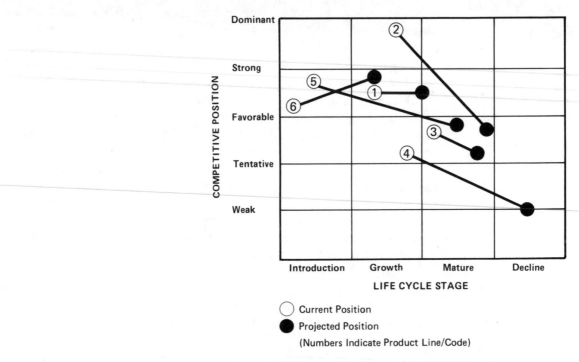

Figure 4.1 Portfolio Business Profile Matrix

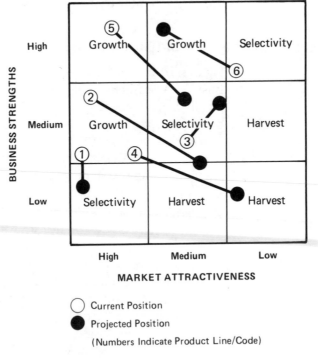

Figure 4.2 Portfolio Business Assessment Matrix

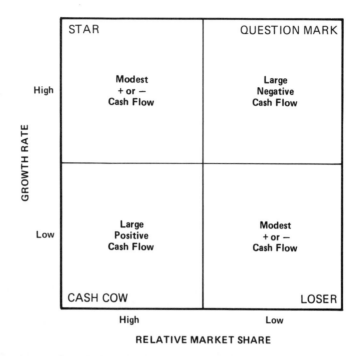

Figure 4.3 **Growth–Share Matrix**

Source: Philip Kotler, *Marketing Management: Analysis, Planning, and Control*, 5th ed. (Englewood Cliffs, N.J.: Prentice-Hall, 1984):43. Copyright 1984. Adapted by permission of Prentice-Hall.

Modified Growth–Share Matrix

The product category matrix or Growth–Share Matrix, shown in Figure 4.3, is usually referred to as "portfolio analysis." When completed, it displays the status and performance of the overall portfolio and suggests which strategy the company should adopt to ensure a strong performance in the future. The information generated by the matrix is used as input into major company strategy planning at the macro level.

The Growth–Share Matrix was developed by the Boston Consulting Group (BCG), and we have adapted this concept to our approach here. Figure 4.4 shows an example of a Growth–Share Matrix using four products. The matrix indicates the following information for each product:

1. Its volume dollar sales (represented by the diameter of the circle). The larger the volume, the larger the circle.
2. Vertical axis shows the growth rate of the market/industry in which the product is competing.
3. Horizontal axis shows the relative market share that the firm's product holds, compared to the share held by the competitor with the largest share.

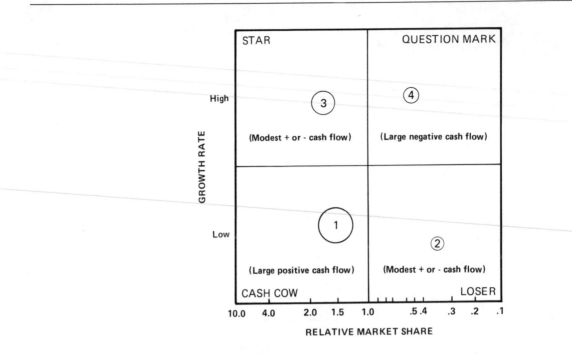

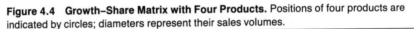

RELATIVE MARKET SHARE

Figure 4.4 **Growth–Share Matrix with Four Products.** Positions of four products are indicated by circles; diameters represent their sales volumes.

Source: B. Heldey, "Strategy and the Business Portfolio," *Long-Range Planning*, February 1977. Copyright 1977 Pergamon Press, Ltd. Adapted by permission of *Long-Range Planning*.

By *growth rate* we mean simply the percentage by which the sales volume of all firms in that particular market has changed during the most recent period for which information is available.

Relative market share is the ratio of the firm's unit sales of a product to the unit sales of the same product by the firm's largest competitor. This is the same as the ratio of the two companies' market shares. For example, if your product A's annual sales were 3.1 million units and the market leader's annual sales were 10 million units, your firm's relative market share for this product would be 0.31 (i.e., 3.1/10 = .31).

However, for markets in which your company is a market leader, your firm will have a relative market share of more than 1.0. Thus, any other company with a ratio of 1.0 would be tied for the lead with your firm.

Relative market share is used in this analysis instead of simply market share since it captures well the relationship of your firm to the leader's share. For instance, your company's 15 percent market share has quite a different meaning if the market leader has a 17 percent share of the total market rather than a 45 percent share. You are much closer to the leader than if it held a 45 percent market share to your 15 percent share.

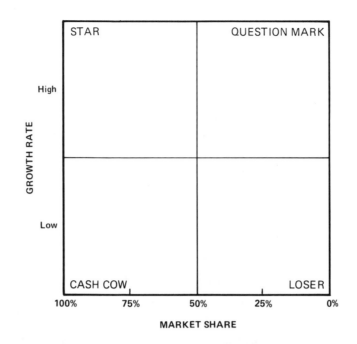

Figure 4.5 Modified Growth–Share Matrix—Simple Market Share

However, you may not always know your competitors' market share nor be able to calculate relative market share for your products. In such cases, you can change the horizontal axis from a log scale to a percentage from 1 to 100 percent, as shown in Figure 4.5, the Modified Growth–Share Matrix. This matrix simply shows your product's market share as a percent and not its relative market share.

In Figure 4.4 we see only the current performance of these products and their markets. As a strategic market planner, you need to think about decisions for the long-range future. Projections can be made for the Growth–Share Matrix by predicting each of the two elements in the figure, although such projections entail some risk, contrary to the certainty of current data.

In a Growth–Share Matrix such as the one shown in Figure 4.4, the value of the horizontal market share dividing line is based on a log scale. The vertical growth rate dividing line is based on the industry/ growth rate associated with these products.

Setting Growth–Share Matrix Values.   Setting the right values for the market share and growth rate dividing lines is strategically important, since they serve as cutoff points in your assessment of the company's portfolio. However, it is up to you to set the points for your particular circumstances. Our example shows 1.0 as the cutoff point for market share, but your firm may have a different point (e.g., 2.0 or 0.5), depending on your firm's objectives. You need to determine whether you like the direction in which your company is moving and, if not, what you need to do to correct it.

In this analysis we're assuming that growth rate and cash use are correlated, as are market share and cash generation. Keep in mind two key assumptions of portfolio analysis:

1. Cash flow from products with high relative market shares will be stronger than cash flow from products with smaller shares.
2. Cash needs for products in faster growing markets will be higher than cash needs for those in slower growing markets.

Interpreting the Modified Growth–Share Matrix

Once you have the matrix plotted, your interpretation of the data will be based on the following:

- Vertical axis—growth rate—represents the level of growth related to a particular product/industry.
- Horizontal axis—market share—indicates the level of market share from a particular product. (Criteria we use to set these dividing lines are merely examples, since these criteria probably would differ in various industries.)
- Margins usually increase with market share because of economies of scale effects.
- Sales growth requires cash input to finance added capacity and working capital. Thus, if market share is maintained, cash input requirements increase with market growth rates.
- An increase in market share usually requires cash input to support increased advertising expenditures, lower prices, and other share-gaining tactics.
- Growth in each market will ultimately slow as the product approaches maturity. Without losing position, cash generated as growth slows down can be reinvested in other products that are still growing.

With these factors in mind, you can see in Figure 4.4 that products below the market share (horizontal) dividing line have modest to strong cash flows from operations. Products above that line have weaker or negative cash flows.

As shown in Figure 4.4, these four product categories have been classified on the basis of their cash flow characteristics as follows:

1. *Cash Cows*—These are products that generate considerable cash, more than can be profitably invested in them. Typically, they

have a dominant share of slowly growing markets. These products provide the cash to pay interest on corporate debt, cover corporate overhead, pay dividends, finance R & D, and provide funds for other products to grow.

2. *Stars*—These products are high-growth, high-share items. They may or may not be self-sufficient in cash flow, depending on whether their cash flow from operations is enough to finance rapid growth.

3. *Question Marks*—These are products with a low share of a fast-growing market. Low market share often means both low profits and weak cash flow from operations because the market is growing rapidly beyond the product. The company must invest large amounts of cash simply to maintain their market share and even greater amounts to increase that share. While the market growth is attractive, considerable cash outlays will be required if the products are ever to gain enough share to become strong members of the portfolio.

4. *Losers*—These products have a low share of slowly growing markets. They neither generate nor require significant amounts of cash. Maintaining market share usually requires reinvestment of their modest cash flow from operations plus some additional capital. Because of their low market share, their profitability is poor. They are unlikely ever to be a significant source of cash.

There is an important exception to this rule, however. It is possible that a new product may be in this cell for a short period during its Introduction Stage before moving to the Question Mark or Star cell during its Growth or Mature Stage. Thus, new products are not treated the same as older Loser products in strategic formulations.

By locating products on a Growth-Share Matrix, you will get a good picture of your portfolio's current health. Over time, the position of your products will move because of market dynamics and your own strategy decisions. The objective of portfolio analysis is to discover the current state of your portfolio as a basis for strategic decisions that will strengthen that portfolio in the future.

Some of the movements of products in the portfolio can be predicted in general terms, depending on the strategies selected and whether the variables are controllable or uncontrollable. For example, movements in the vertical direction (i.e., rate of total market growth) are largely beyond the firm's control and must be anticipated when developing your strategy.

A firm that selects only a share-maintaining strategy for its portfolio will find that eventually all products become either Cash Cows or Losers, and more likely fall into the Loser category. Whether they become Cash Cows or Losers, however, depends on the market share

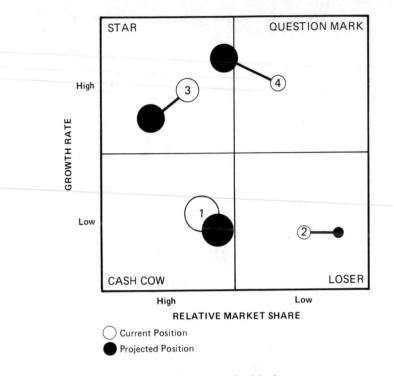

Figure 4.6 Growth–Share Matrix—Future Positioning

Source: Luck/Ferrell, *Marketing Strategy and Plans*, 2nd ed. (Englewood Cliffs, N.J.: Prentice-Hall, 1985):77. Adapted by permission of Prentice-Hall.

they hold before market growth slows, usually before the products reach their late mature life cycle stage.

Likewise, Question Marks ultimately become Losers unless the company invests enough during the Growth Stage to shift the product into the Star category. Stars ensure the company's future because they will become Cash Cows as market growth slows and investment needs decline.

Future positioning and sales volume are given in Figure 4.6. Shaded circles represent the data three years from now, while lines indicate the desirable future direction. Funds are pumped from the Cash Cows to strengthen the competitive positions of the Question Marks and Stars and to develop and acquire other new products.

Form 4: Modified Growth–Share Matrix enables you to see the current and projected positions of product lines in a macro or portfolio view. By mapping your own product lines on the form, you can determine which products are following a "success sequence," and which products may need to be repositioned or eliminated from your portfolio.

All the matrices we have discussed in this section will enable you to see all products on an equal plane and will help you to identify

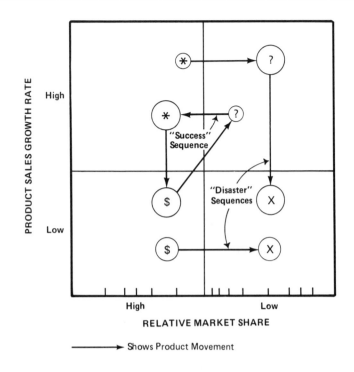

Figure 4.7 Product Dynamics Matrix

Source: "The Product Portfolio" (Boston: The Boston Consulting Group, 1970): Perspectives, No. 66.

which products in the portfolio need to be repositioned. The Product Dynamics Matrix, discussed below, can be used to illustrate successful product repositioning strategies.

Product Dynamics Matrix

The Product Dynamics Matrix, illustrated in Figure 4.7, shows the optimal repositioning of a product from one cell on the matrix to another. The cells we use in this matrix are equivalent to those used in the Growth–Share Matrix. The objective of this chart is to illustrate a success sequence that a product can follow to gain market share and increase cash flow. Once the product has been positioned on the Growth–Share Matrix, you can formulate specific strategies on the basis of the "success sequence."

It is important at this point to understand a key principle of the macro view. With market growth largely uncontrollable in most instances, portfolio analysis becomes a way to develop a market share strategy for individual products. You are going to use all the data you have generated so far and begin to determine which strategy or strategies will help you to move your portfolio in the right direction to achieve your overall company objectives.

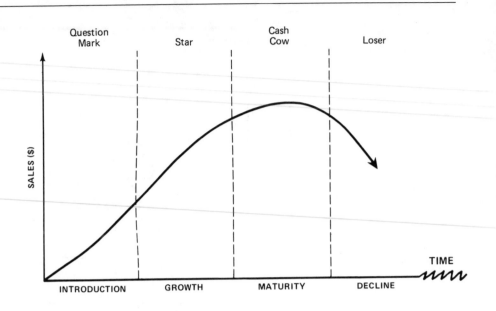

Figure 4.8 Success Sequence and Product Life Cycle

Success Sequence.   The basis of a sound, long-term strategy is to use cash generated by Cash Cows to fund market share increases for Question Mark products in which the company has a *strong* competitive advantage. You will be able to identify such products through your competitive analysis, product evaluation, and matrices. If successful, this strategy will produce new Stars that, in turn, will become the company's future Cash Cows. This success sequence is illustrated in Figure 4.7.

On the other hand, the Question Mark product with a *weak* competitive position is a liability to the firm. The product should be allowed to remain in the portfolio only if the company spends little or no cash to maintain its position. This strategy will cause the product to become a Loser eventually. Losers should be retained only if they contribute some positive cash flow and do not tie up funds that could be used more profitably elsewhere. At some point, the company must consider eliminating Loser products from the portfolio.

Product Life Cycle and the Success Sequence.   In many respects, the success sequence is closely associated with the movement of a product along its life cycle, as shown in Figure 4.8. Product categories relate closely to product life cycle stages, another reason it is important to identify each product's position along the life cycle curve. Thus, life cycle planning techniques also can be used in strategy formulation, as discussed in Chapter 6.

We should mention as well that because the Growth–Share Matrix represents performance only in the most recent period, either total category volume or a product's market share may fluctuate temporarily and cross one of the dividing lines for that moment. As a result, you may be plotting only a short-term effect for some products falling close to the dividing lines. However, it would be wise to investigate whether even this slight movement might have some attractive strategic possibilities for your company.

Common Pitfalls in Strategic Planning

Unfortunately, many managements pursue "disaster sequences" instead of the success sequence described above. For example, a company may allow a Star product's market share to erode to that of a Question Mark. Unless the strategy is reversed or corrected, the product will ultimately become a Loser.

Companies may also overinvest in Cash Cows, or they may try to save ailing Cash Cows by pumping funds into them. A better strategy would be to reposition these products according to the success sequence via such factors as product differentiation, market segmentation, and product enhancement. If firms overinvest in Cash Cows, they may underinvest in Question Marks. Instead of becoming Stars, these products eventually tumble into the Loser category.

Some companies spread their resources too thinly among products rather than focusing their funds to achieve the maximum performance from the strongest or most promising products. Even a smaller number of products can still provide enough diversification to reduce a company's risk in the market.

Look over the disaster sequence portfolios presented in Figures 4.9 and 4.10 and study their mistakes. What makes these portfolios vulnerable to loss of market share and profits?

Product and Portfolio Analysis of Competitors

We strongly recommend that you do a product evaluation and matrices analysis of your strongest competitors' products and product lines after you have completed the analysis for your own company. By superimposing these competitive matrices on your own, you can spot vulnerabilities, strengths and weaknesses, and opportunities more easily.

Companies with the best product track records routinely analyze their competitors' products as well as their own products. They have more accurate data on which to base their strategic marketing plans.

In the following chapter, we show you how to identify problems and opportunities that turn up in your product positioning and portfolio analysis.

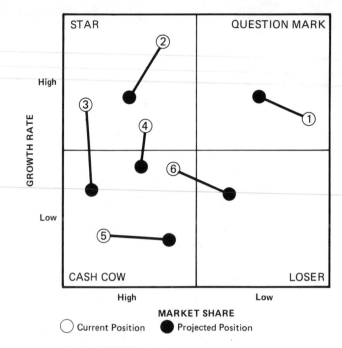

Figure 4.9   Growth–Share Matrix—Disaster Sequence in Long Run

1. Products 5 and 6 will become Losers in the long run.
2. Product 1, the only new product, is a slow grower as shown by the growth rate; it is the only product that will be supporting the company's future growth in the long run.
3. Products 3 and 4 will become Cash Cows in the future, but Product 4 will not remain so for long if it follows the path of Products 5 and 6.
4. Product 2 is losing market share rapidly.
5. Product 6, as a Loser, will still be in the portfolio, but its position will rapidly worsen.

In the short run, if projections had not been made as depicted in the chart, management may believe that the portfolio looks sound with its Cash Cows, growth rate, and the like. But the long-run view shows a firm that will decline in profitability, market share, and growth rate. The firm is following the success sequence only to the point where products are moving counterclockwise, but they are not regenerating Cash Cows nor introducing new products. As a result, in the long run, if the firm continues its present course, it will have few Cash Cows or Stars, no Question Marks, and many Losers.

Basically, the firm has three choices: (1) regenerate Cash Cows back to Question Marks, (2) introduce new products, and (3) reexamine its company and product strategies and its company mission.

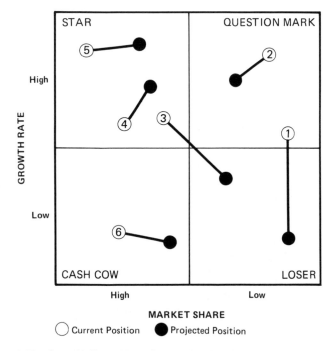

Figure 4.10 Growth–Share Matrix—"Lost" Portfolio

1. Product 1 is falling from introductory category to Loser position. Either the product is a complete failure, market research was in error, financing was not available, or strategic objectives were poorly planned.
2. Product 5 is following a disaster sequence, moving from Star position to Question Mark, again probably through poor strategy.
3. Product 3 is falling from high growth to Loser category.
4. Product 6 is not being regenerated. Its position as Cash Cow is eroding to Loser category.

The basic problem of this portfolio is that little or no planning is being done in this firm. Perhaps the firm views products on an individual basis without projecting their movements to see the total portfolio effect on whatever plan they have.

It's more likely that management has never mapped out the product portfolio. Management's attitude is *reactive*, that is, no future projections have been made, or they have been made in a product-by-product vacuum without considering the other product strategies. There is no interaction among products. The company has an extremely short-sighted view of its products and of its future.

Summary

Since we have covered considerable ground in Chapters 3 and 4, it may be helpful to recap the main points of product positioning and portfolio analysis.

- The primary purpose of the Product Evaluation Questionnaire and the matrices up to the Product Dynamics Matrix is to assess a product's position in terms of competition, market share, and market growth.
- Each matrix, by itself, provides part of the information you need to develop marketing mix strategies for the marketing plan. When all the data generated during the analysis process are taken into account, final product strategies can be devised.
- The flow of information from these various matrices can be summarized as follows:

(Chapter 3)

1. The Business Profile Matrix provides data to develop marketing mix strategies based on the position of the product in its life cycle and its market attractiveness.

2. The Business Assessment Matrix uses the product life cycle data together with situational factors to determine the attractiveness of the market and whether internal business strengths can make the product a strong competitor. This matrix also indicates whether the product should grow, stabilize, or be harvested.

(Chapter 4)

3. The Portfolio Business Profile Matrix and Portfolio Business Assessment Matrix are used to consolidate individual product positions to map a portfolio of the product line.

4. The Growth–Share Matrix plots a company's product line in terms of products' growth rates (cash use) and market shares (cash generation).

5. The Product Dynamics Matrix illustrates the success and disaster sequences, suggesting how to reposition products to achieve company goals.

- The data collected from the Business Profile Matrix and Business Assessment Matrix are used to develop product marketing mix strategies in order to achieve the objectives of these product strategies.
- The Growth–Share Matrix displays the status and performance of the overall portfolio and can suggest which strategy the company should adopt to ensure a strong performance in the near future. The information generated by the matrix is used as input into company strategic planning at the macro level.

- The overall objective of the product portfolio analysis is to maximize return on investment on the basis of products' cash flow. All products are mapped on the Portfolio Business Profile Matrix, Portfolio Business Assessment Matrix, and Growth–Share Matrix. This will help you to determine the overall health of the company's portfolio now and in the near future to be sure the firm is following a success sequence.

- The Product Dynamics Matrix is also of major importance in strategy development since it provides the big picture of the direction in which your company's products should be moving. By using the success sequence as a guide to reposition products and to increase cash flow, you can determine specific product strategies.

Sample Case   Getting the Big Picture

Haines now had a profile for each of DataStar's products, including AutoDrive which had been shown as a strong, potentially high-profit item for the firm. Through the work he and his marketing team had done so far, the data could now be used for strategy formulation. In the future, as the team gained more experience refining the data and the analytic methods used, the results would become increasingly more valuable and accurate for market planning.

At this point, Haines needed to see how all the product lines were positioned and projected to move in one macro or portfolio view. This would tell him which lines were following the success, or the disaster, sequence. Since DataStar already has a problem with declining sales and market share, the portfolio view would help pinpoint the reasons. This information could then be used to formulate improved objectives and strategies for the marketing plan. The portfolio view would also help managers set capital and expense allocations at the individual product plan level.

His marketing team plotted all products on the Modified Growth–Share Matrix, setting the values for the horizontal and vertical axes. Haines then arranged a meeting with the three partners to show them the results of his work to date.

Haines pointed to the Growth–Share Matrix. "With this chart, we can assess each product line to determine which ones represent investment opportunities, which ones should supply investment funds, and which ones should be eliminated from the portfolio. The information will serve as the basis for developing our corporate marketing objectives and strategies.

"Our overall objective is to get the best performance from all product lines while at the same time keeping the cash flow in balance.

We don't want to go to capital markets for more funds unless it's absolutely necessary.

"I've done a Portfolio Business Profile and Portfolio Business Assessment and found that the results were consistent with what we plotted on the Growth–Share Matrix. The marketing team determined that the industry growth rate on average for the seven product lines is 9 percent."

Koster broke in. "Why are you using a Modified Growth–Share Matrix instead of relative market share as your basis?"

"The modified matrix is easier to use at the beginning when the staff is learning the technique. When they get more proficient and understand the internal and external environment better, we can switch to a relative market share basis for the matrix."

Price was the most enthusiastic of the three when he saw the portfolio view of DataStar's products.

"I don't know about the rest of you," he said, "but this is the first time I've seen all our products on a single graph and on an equal plane at one time. One thing I want to know: What if our products were in different industries?"

"They couldn't be compared directly; we'd have to make up separate portfolios for each line of business."

Simic waved his hand for silence. "All I want to know is what's the bottom line on this? What is it telling us to do?"

Haines handed out copies of his summary. "I've itemized the important information the portfolio reveals and what we need to do to correct or take advantage of each product's position."

Modified Growth–Share Matrix (Form 4)

Product: __AutoDrive__   Date: _____

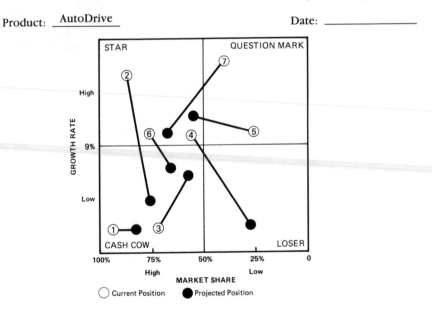

Conclusions from Modified
Growth–Share Matrix—All Product Lines

The matrix shows a generally dynamic and well-managed portfolio, with Product Line 3 being regenerated back to a growth position and Product Line 5 following a success sequence. Product Line 7, Auto-Drive, is forecasted to follow a success sequence and so far has conformed to projected growth as forecast by the marketing team. This product should be a high-revenue, high-market share item for Data-Star.

However, the matrix also shows a number of problems that pinpoint the reasons for DataStar's sales and market share losses. These problems must be resolved or they will eventually result in the deterioration of the entire product portfolio.

1. Product Line 1 must be checked to see whether it can be stabilized or regenerated using a product differentiation or substitution strategy. If Product Line 1 must be replaced within three years, the Vice President of Marketing should contact R & D so they can either enhance or replace the products in this line. Until then, they can be used as cash providers for other growing products.

2. Product Line 2 has a growth rate and market share that appear to be falling too fast. However, the marketing team believes that the product manager's projections for this line are too pessimistic. Revised projections indicate that these products should not decline so rapidly. They should fall only to the top of the Cash Cow range, generating more revenue for the firm.

3. Product Line 4 is following a disaster sequence. It has no planned updates to keep it current with competitors, which are overtaking this item. There is not enough time to upgrade and reposition this line to catch up with the competition. The marketing team recommends that the firm drop these products.

4. Product Line 6 is poorly managed and has no overall marketing strategy guiding its growth, only day-to-day tactical responses. The marketing team estimates that, with sufficient funds, this line can be regenerated to give it a longer product life. Repositioned properly, it can regain market share. As a Cash Cow, these products can make up some of their lost revenues and possibly compensate for the elimination of Product Line 4.

Summary of Strategic Implications

As shown on the graph, Product Lines 4 and 6 are responsible for DataStar's current decline in sales and market share. Two years ago, these products had high profit margins, good market share, and revenues equalling 36 percent of DataStar's total sales. At present, they represent only 14 percent. Even AutoDrive and other products cannot make up the 22 percent loss.

This decline is the result of DataStar's lack of an overall marketing strategy and planning process. The firm had no plan to meet the competitive challenges to its major product lines and consequently lost customers and market share to its main competitors.

In addition, DataStar is investing too much money in Product Line 1 for the return being generated. Product Line 2, on the other hand, is underinvested. It has low revenues but very high profit margins and needs more cash investment to make it grow. These conditions also reflect the lack of adequate planning. There has been no method for determining which products should be funded and which ones should be gradually eliminated.

We need to develop objectives and strategies to get all product lines on a success sequence and drop the ones that cannot be regenerated. Between now and the next three years, more new products and regenerated products must be located in the Question Mark (Introduction Stage) cell. This strategy will ensure that DataStar continues to grow and regains its position as a leading-edge company.

After the three partners had a chance to review the summary, Haines said, "We have one more step in the environmental assessment before we're through. That's to start plotting our main competitor's products against ours so we can see the competition's strengths, weaknesses, strategies, and so on. Afterward, we can move on to identify DataStar's key problems and opportunities that turned up in our data-gathering process. Then we'll be ready to set our marketing objectives and strategies."

"Looks like a great job so far," Price said.

Even Simic had to agree.

CHAPTER FIVE

Step 4: Problem and Opportunity Analysis

Introduction

At this point, we take a look at one of the additional benefits of the planning process—identifying problems and opportunities in the early stages. While we will not go into this analysis in great detail, we will give you practical methods to uncover and analyze your firm's basic problems and opportunities.

It is not always easy to recognize problems before they become major issues. In firms of all sizes, managers frequently make the mistake of believing that minor problems will correct themselves without intervention.

On the other hand, marketing managers may just as easily fail to spot potential opportunities during the environmental assessment process. They may lose the chance to make an early entry into a particular niche in the market, differentiate their product, or in some way edge out the competition.

In this chapter, we examine the data you developed in the questionnaires and matrices to help you pinpoint potential problems and opportunities. Some of them will be obvious; others may be more hidden. The point is to identify them now so that action steps can be designed and included as part of the marketing plan.

Identifying Problems

A *problem* can be defined as a question or situation that presents uncertainty, perplexity, or difficulty. In practical terms, it is something that could prevent you from achieving your company's goals and requires your attention and correction.

To spot a problem in its early stage, you must have some idea of what to look for and where to look. We recommend you start with the following:

1. Determine whether any variances from previous plans have occurred, such as these:
   - Decreased market share.
   - Higher inventories.
   - Increased accounts receivables.
   - Increased customer returns.
   - Lower profit margins.

2. Determine what obstacles are preventing you from reaching any of your company goals.

   External factors may include these:
   - Raw material shortages.
   - Increased competition.
   - Increased returns of products because of continuing quality control problems.
   - Price competitiveness.
   - Increased regulatory threat.
   - Substitution threat.
   - Poor product positioning.
   - Marketing to wrong customer target segment.
   - Poor distribution structure.

   Internal factors may include these:
   - A more risk-averse management.
   - Breadth of product applications.
   - Below-average marketing research.
   - Poor planning.
   - Insufficient funds.
   - Low product servicing.
   - Business plan and marketing plan not integrated.

When filling out Form 5: Problem Analysis at the end of this chapter, make sure you include all problems regardless of size. You can always eliminate some items later. Keep in mind that the obvious weak points may not do the most damage; often it's the problems you might be tempted to disregard in your environmental analysis that can create a crisis.

Analyzing Problems

After listing the problems, the next step is to analyze them. Follow this procedure:

1. Rank the problems according to their importance to your firm. For example, how critical is one product's slight drop in market share in terms of achieving the company's objectives? Is the lack of competitor information of little or of major importance? You can use a numeric value system or a weighted system in ranking problems.

2. Determine whether the problems are industry or company problems. Are the problems stemming from conditions in the industry—recession, shakeout, technological changes, foreign competition? Or are they primarily caused by factors in the company—overexpansion in the market, management changes, too broad or too narrow a product line?

3. Examine the problems and determine whether two or more share a single cause. For example, declining market share, slowing growth, and falling profits may all be the result of a failure to invest enough funds in maintaining a product's position. By correcting the cause, several problems are solved at once.

On the other hand, the problems may all be due to a shift in consumer taste that renders your product obsolete. There may be no way to salvage the product, since the underlying cause is beyond the firm's control. This point leads us to the fourth step.

4. Separate the problems into those that can be solved and those that, for various reasons, are unsolvable. Problems that can be solved usually are those over which you have some control. The control may be over price, market share, breadth of product line, or other factors that lie within your power to change. A solvable problem may also reveal a hidden marketing opportunity.

Unsolvable problems are generally those over which you have little or no control. You must examine these problems closely to determine their effect on the firm. If a product is losing market share because of changing economic conditions, it may be better to consider dropping the product rather than pumping more cash into it in an attempt to reposition the product.

Even if you have no control over a problem, make sure you write it down. By stating the problem in writing, you help to ensure that it won't be ignored in the planning process. Besides, if conditions change, you may be able to do something about the problem after all.

5. List action steps that can be taken to solve problems. After each problem that you determine can be solved, list the action steps your firm can take to correct it. Perhaps you can restructure your pricing system, or you may be able to target a different consumer segment to rebuild sales. The action steps you design can be incorporated into the marketing plan.

6. Determine whether solving the problem will lead to meaningful and favorable change in your current position. This step ensures that you will focus on significant problems in the short term rather than concentrate on problems that may arise in the more distant future.

The purpose of these steps is to get beyond symptoms—declining profits, decreasing market share—to the core problem, which may be a shift in consumer taste, a strategic error on the company's part, or increased competition in the market. The core problem, if solvable, is the one you want to list in your marketing plan, along with your proposed action steps to address it.

Turning Problems into Opportunities

The final step is to review your list of problems and determine whether you can turn some of them into opportunities. For example, you may discover that the slight decline in sales of a certain product is caused by a subtle change in consumer taste (style or color change). If your competitors have similar products, you can probably assume they are also experiencing the same decline. But they may not have noticed the trend. You can be sure that the moment they do, they will begin working on a solution—fast—to recover market share.

If you make the change in your product first, you can turn the problem into a short-term market window and possibly achieve a substantial market share gain.

Problems do not always signal that something is wrong; they can be opportunities in disguise. By making problem identification and analysis a regular part of your planning process, you will be able to detect the opportunity hidden in the problem and help your firm stay ahead of the competition.

Identifying Opportunities

A firm needs more than good problem analysis to continue to grow. You must also identify and take advantage of opportunities. To sustain a strong pattern of growth, you need to analyze these opportunities in light of your company's mission and business plan, objectives, and resources.

As in problem analysis, your first step is to identify all opportunities, no matter how slight or improbable they may seem at first. State the opportunities in writing as specifically as you can.

When looking for opportunities, consider those that are associated with the following:

- Your specific company strengths.
- Product advantages.
- Changing consumer life styles.
- New technologies.
- Market coverage.
- Financial and resource advantages.
- Distribution structure.
- Organization structure.
- Changing customer wants and needs.
- Geographic coverage.
- New applications of existing products.
- Improvement in production or service facilities.

Analyzing Opportunities

Once you have developed your list, you will need to look carefully at each opportunity to determine which ones are worth pursuing. Follow these steps in your analysis.

1. Rank the opportunities in order of their importance or contribution value to your firm. Each firm has limited resources that restrict how many opportunities can be pursued. List the opportunities you find in their order of importance or value to your firm.

2. Determine which opportunities are most compatible with your corporation. Compatibility is judged on the basis of growth, market share, business plan, and mission. Questions you should ask in determining good corporate fit include these:

- Does the firm want to capitalize on products that complement the current product line?
- Does the firm want to diversify into totally new areas?
- Does the firm want to become a market leader or merely to increase or maintain market share?
- Does the firm have the resources and skills necessary to pursue the opportunity?

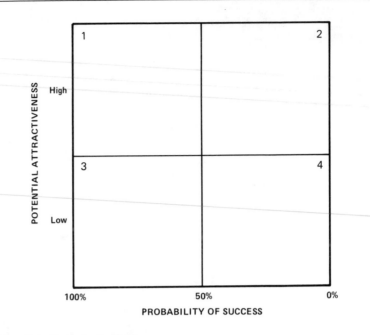

Figure 5.1   Opportunity Matrix

Source: Adapted from "The Product Portfolio" (Boston: The Boston Consulting Group, 1970): Perspectives, No. 66.

The opportunities that the firm finally selects should be completely in line with the direction and mission of the firm as stated in the business plan.

3. Assign numeric values to opportunities. When you have ranked the opportunities, you will need to assess them. An opportunity can be assessed in terms of two dimensions: (1) attractiveness to the firm and (2) the firm's probability of success in developing the opportunity. Assign a value to each opportunity for each of these two dimensions. You might want to rank opportunities 1 to 10 for market attractiveness. Probability of success can be set at 0 to 100 percent.

4. Plot opportunities on an Opportunity Matrix. Figure 5.1 illustrates an Opportunity Matrix with four cells. To plot opportunities on the matrix, look at the values for the two dimensions you have assigned each opportunity; then map the opportunity in the appropriate cell. The instructions for Form 6: Opportunity and Resource Analysis show you how to plot your own matrix.

The opportunity matrix is interpreted as follows:

• Opportunities that fall in Cell 1 have the highest attractiveness and probability of success. You would design specific strategies (action steps) to realize them and include those strategies in your marketing plan.

- Opportunities that fall in Cells 2 and 3 are worth monitoring, although you would not develop specific steps to achieve them at this point.

- Opportunities that fall in Cell 4 have little attractiveness and little chance of success. They should be dropped from consideration.

The Sample Case shows a list of weighted opportunities and a completed matrix.

5. Develop action steps to realize potential opportunities. After each opportunity, list the action steps your firm must take to achieve it.

Identifying Resources

Once you have selected the opportunities worth developing, you must determine whether your firm has the resources needed to realize them. Resource analysis will help you to focus on practical results and to keep your planning realistic in terms of your company's strengths and limitations. Always ask the question "What is it *possible* for us to do?" versus "What would we *like* to do?"

In identifying company resources, consider the following areas:

- Does the firm possess adequate financial resources to support a new marketing opportunity?

- Are there qualified personnel to manufacture, sell, and manage the new opportunity?

- Is there enough capacity to produce the necessary quantities to meet projected demand?

- Can basic raw materials be acquired easily?

- Can the product be priced to reach the target market and still contribute a profit?

- Can an effective advertising program be developed to reach the target market?

- Are current distribution channels adequate to channel the product to its dealers or end-users?

If you find yourself answering "no" to most of these questions, then even an excellent opportunity may have to be discarded because your firm doesn't have the necessary resources to develop it. Conversely, if an opportunity is somewhat risky but the firm has adequate resources, you may decide to take a calculated risk and pursue the opportunity. Some factors such as available capacity and price structure are difficult to estimate in a rough analysis. For this reason, we have not included them on the Opportunity Analysis form.

The analyses presented in this chapter will give you a good overview of the problems and potential opportunities of your firm. You will need to do more detailed work to develop specific tactical plans to handle the problems and potentials you find.

Study the Sample Case below, then fill out Form 5: Problem Analysis, and Form 6: Opportunity and Resource Analysis. Remember to keep an open mind when examining your data for problems or opportunities. Don't assume that you know what they are or where to find them. Pay particular attention to slight changes in product performance or market conditions. You may discover that even minor problems or opportunities can be turned into the competitive edge your firm needs.

Summary

- Problem and opportunity analysis is a practical means of identifying even minor problems and opportunities early in the planning process. Steps can then be taken to minimize these problems and maximize opportunities.

- A problem can be identified as a question or situation that presents uncertainty, perplexity, or difficulty to a firm. In practical terms, it is something that may prevent a company from achieving its goals and that requires attention and correction. The purpose of the analysis is to get beyond symptoms to the core problem.

- To spot a problem in its early stage, start with the following: (1) Determine whether any variances from previous plans have occurred and (2) determine which obstacles are preventing you from reaching any of your company's goals.

- Analyze problems using the following procedure: (1) Rank the problems according to their importance to your firm, (2) determine whether the problems are industry or company problems, (3) examine them and determine whether two or more share a single cause, (4) separate the problems into those that can be solved and those that are unsolvable, (5) list action steps that can be taken to solve the problems, (6) determine whether solving the problem will lead to significant and favorable change in your current position, and (7) determine which problems can be turned into opportunities.

- To analyze opportunities, follow these steps: (1) Rank the opportunities in order of their importance or contribution value to your firm, (2) determine which opportunities are most compatible with your corporation, (3) assign numeric values to opportunities (attractiveness and probability of success), (4) plot opportunities on the Opportunity Matrix, (5) develop action steps to realize potential opportunities, and (6) determine whether your firm has the resources to develop opportunities you identify.

Sample Case
DataStar's Problems and Opportunities

Haines discussed the portfolio view of DataStar's seven product lines with all concerned managers. He gained additional information regarding why the products were behaving the way the product positioning and portfolio matrices projected. The managers seemed more genuinely involved in the process this time around, and some even expressed their appreciation for what they had learned from the product evaluation and portfolio analysis.

Haines then called his marketing team together to begin the problem and opportunity analysis for DataStar's seven product lines. "You can use a two-step, systematic approach to this process," Haines told the team. "First, determine whether any variance from previous plans, statistics, market share data, or sales figures has occurred. Second, determine what internal and external obstacles are preventing DataStar from achieving its current goals."

Haines gave the marketing team Forms 5 and 6 to fill out for each product line. He instructed them to analyze the problems they uncovered as follows:

- Rank the problems according to their importance to the firm.
- Determine whether they are industry or company problems.
- Examine each problem in detail to determine whether two or more of them share a single cause.
- Separate problems into solvable or unsolvable.
- List preliminary actions that can be taken to solve problems.
- Determine whether solving the problem will lead to meaningful and favorable change in the product's market position.
- Review the final list of problems and determine whether some of them can be turned into opportunities.

When the team turned in their analysis for each product, Haines was particularly interested in the completed Form 5 for AutoDrive (shown at the end of the Sample Case). The marketing team had uncovered the following problems:

1. DataStar's major competitor is entering a joint agreement with two large computer manufacturers to purchase the competitor's products and possibly produce them under a private label. This agreement will

provide the competitor with increased market share and an immediate national distribution system. In contrast, DataStar's distribution system is still one year away from achieving national coverage.

2. Sales staff training is a problem for DataStar and competitors alike. DataStar has adequate sales staff, but they need to be trained to sell AutoDrive to the national target markets. Developing and instituting the training program could take up to two months. A time lag that long might allow competitors to catch up on sales, installation, and service.

3. DataStar does not have an alliance with a large computer manufacturer, which may cause the firm to lose customers and market share to its competitor.

Once the problem analysis was completed, Haines instructed his staff to take a similar look at the opportunities. In their analysis they would do the following:

- Rank opportunities according to their importance or contribution value to the firm.

- Determine which opportunities are most compatible with the firm.

- Assign numeric values to opportunities indicating their level of attractiveness to DataStar and their probability of success. Plot these opportunities on the Opportunity Matrix.

- Determine which of the available opportunities DataStar has the resources to pursue.

The marketing team filled out Form 6 for all product lines and turned in their findings to Haines. He saw that for AutoDrive, the team had identified several important opportunities (Form 6 is shown following the Sample Case):

1. Form an alliance with a major computer manufacturer to increase market share and gain wider and faster distribution for AutoDrive.

2. Develop distribution channels more rapidly, either through the alliance mentioned earlier or through the potential acquisition of competitors.

3. Increase funds for sales force and service employee training to teach them about AutoDrive's features and specifications.

4. Be flexible in pricing structure. Although it is not the best way to increase market share, DataStar may have to change its philosophy on pricing, particularly if the competitor offers a similar, lower-priced hard disk drive. However, the firm must give this approach careful consideration. DataStar's high-quality reputation among customers may serve to counteract the competitor's pricing strategy. Customers

may buy AutoDrive even with its higher price tag because they know that they are also buying the company's service and installation skills.

Haines was satisfied with the team's work and told them that they now had enough information to begin developing marketing objectives and strategies for the final marketing plan. He had one word of caution, however. "Keep in mind," he advised them, "that we need to consult the department heads, product managers, and their staffs at every step in the planning process. We want them involved as we go along, so the final plan is *their* plan, not just ours."

The marketing team agreed although, Haines thought, they were a bit reluctant.

Form 5   Problem Analysis

Product: ___AutoDrive___   Date: _____

Problems

1. List all problems:

(1) Competition will have joint agreement with two of the largest computer manufacturers.

DataStar currently has none.

(2) National distribution system will take one year to implement.

(3) Because of joint agreement, competitor will have access to large manufacturer's resources:

capital, new technology, increased distributor channels, etc.

(4) It will take two months to fully train DataStar's sales staff.

2. a. Rank problems in order of their importance to your firm:

(2), (1), (4), (3)

b. List problems that share a single cause:

Problems	Cause
(1) National coverage is desired but at present is mostly local.	During testing phase we did not train sales force nor did we pursue computer manufacturers aggressively. Instead, we waited for manufacturers to come to us.
(2) Competitors are entering into joint agreement with two of the largest computer manufacturers and will be able to use their distribution system at low start-up cost.	

3. a. Industry-related problems:

(1) No firmly set standards for product (i.e., interface, protocols) especially for mini- and microcomputers.

(2) Very fast-paced industry, short product life span.

   b. Company-related problems:

(1) Sales force

(2) Service and distribution

(3) Pricing

(4) R & D expense

(5) Poor planning

4. a. Problems that can be solved (over which you have some control):

(1) Industry-related—must make equipment compatible with that of large computer manufacturers.

(2) Lower the learning curve for sales force by increasing training funds.

(3) Pricing must be more flexible to match competitors.

b. Problems that cannot be solved (over which you have little or no control):

(1) Funds available to competitor from its alliance with large manufacturer.

(2) Competition has products compatible with largest computer companies.

(3) R & D is costly, difficult to estimate funds needed to stay ahead of competition.

5. Action steps that can be taken to solve problems:

Problem	Action Steps
(1) Industry norms.	(1) Talk to major manufacturers who will use the product and develop standards.
(2) Decrease learning curve.	(2) Increase training efforts and available funds.
(3) Build distribution channels.	(3) Increase funds allocated for distribution or acquisition of competitors.
(4) Pricing.	(4) May have to lower fixed ROI as stated in company objectives to be competitive in short run and then raise ROI in the long run as company becomes more competitive.

6. Problems that can be turned into opportunities:

Problem	Possible Opportunity
(1) Industry norms.	(1) Make our equipment compatible with large computer manufacturer and form an alliance with them to increase market share and distribution network. Our product may set industry standard.
(2) Pricing.	(2) Decrease price and increase market share in short run, since we are basically alone in current market.

(3) Distribution.	(3) Increase market share and exposure of firm to large customers by increasing distribution structure or acquiring competitors and finding new users of products.
(4) Sales force.	(4) Increase the skill levels of sales reps to increase distribution, sales, revenue. Consider expanding sales forces; introduce telemarketing.

Form 6   Opportunity and Resource Analysis

Product: _____AutoDrive_____   Date: _____

Opportunities

1. List all potential opportunities:

(1) Form an alliance with manufacturers to help set industry standards.

(2) Make pricing more flexible to increase market share and to compete effectively.

(3) Build a larger distribution system for national coverage.

(4) Increase skills of current sales force; consider expansion of sales force for increased customer contact; introduce telemarketing.

(5) Keep increasing R & D program to make company a leader, not a follower; however, funds may be short.

2. Determine which opportunities are most compatible with your firm:

(1), (3), (4), and (5)

3. Assess opportunities in terms of attractiveness to firm and probability of success:

Opportunity	Attractiveness to firm*	Probability of success
(1) Industry alliance.	10	.60
(2) Distribution system.	7	.80
(3) Sales force.	7	.60
(4) Pricing.	2	.90
(5) Increase R & D.	6	.30

*Scale is from 1 to 10, with 10 indicating greatest attractiveness to the firm.

4. Plot opportunities on Opportunity Matrix.

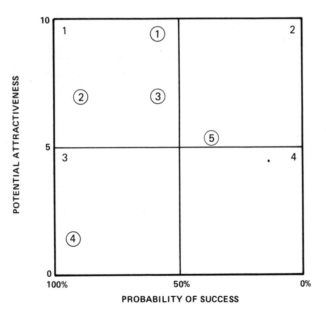

5. List opportunities selected and action steps developed to realize them:

(1) Industry alliance.   (1) Meet with other manufacturing executives; set up mutual

R & D agreements.

(2) Distribution.   (2) Increase funds to build up distribution channels. Increase

funds to reduce time required to expand capacity and to

investigate potential acquisitions.

(3) Sales force.   (3) Increase funds for training to lower learning curve.

Resources

1. Financial resources available to develop opportunities:

Opportunities	Financial Resources
(1) Industry alliance.	
(2) Distribution.	Available for all three.
(3) Sales force.	

2. Personnel needed to develop opportunities:

a. Management:

None.

b. Research and Development:

Add two engineers.

c. Manufacturing:

Study required to determine optimal capacity.

d. Sales:

Prepare study to determine whether sales force needs to be increased and by what percent.

e. Marketing:

Increase marketing personnel by 7 percent.

3. Raw materials needed:

Raw Material	Difficult to source	Moderately difficult	Moderately easy	Easy to source
Electronic components			X	

4. Advertising effort needed to develop opportunities:

Opportunities	Advertising Effort
(1) Industry alliance.	(1) Depends on alliance agreement.
(2) Distribution.	(2) None.
(3) Sales force.	(3) Brochure, direct mail-direct reply, telemarketing, trade publications.
(4) Pricing.	(4) Trade publications; direct sales.

5. Distribution channels needed:

Opportunities	Distribution Channels
(1) Industry alliance.	(1) Depends on alliance agreement; may be able to piggyback on manufacturers' channels.

PART THREE

Developing the Plan

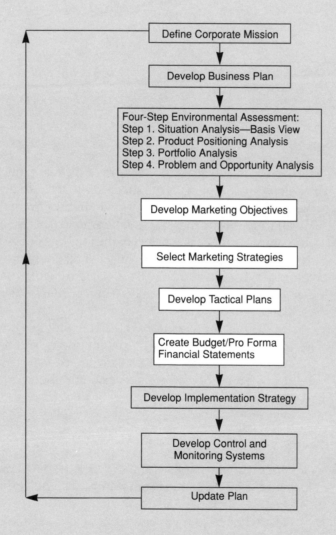

Define Corporate Mission

Develop Business Plan

Four-Step Environmental Assessment:
Step 1. Situation Analysis—Basis View
Step 2. Product Positioning Analysis
Step 3. Portfolio Analysis
Step 4. Problem and Opportunity Analysis

Develop Marketing Objectives

Select Marketing Strategies

Develop Tactical Plans

Create Budget/Pro Forma Financial Statements

Develop Implementation Strategy

Develop Control and Monitoring Systems

Update Plan

CHAPTER SIX

Marketing Objectives

Introduction

Marketing objectives are at the core of the marketing plan. All preceding steps lead to them and all succeeding steps are designed to achieve them. This process is carried out within the context of the Corporate Mission and Business Plan. It can be argued that strategies or tactics are more important because they get the job done, but objectives provide the link between the corporate level of planning and each department plan. Sound marketing objectives will also enable you to select the best marketing strategies to position your products successfully. (We review strategies in Chapter 7.)

In the first three sections of this chapter, we cover balancing objectives, listing their underlying assumptions, and developing criteria for testing objectives. The final two sections provide examples of good marketing objectives and examine the need for contingency plans.

Balancing Objectives

Objectives provide targets for the direction and guidance of marketing strategies. They should identify an actual end result to be achieved within a specific time frame.

Marketing requires a number of objectives to fulfill the Corporate Mission. You will need objectives for the following:

- Existing products and services in current and future markets.
- Disinvestment in unprofitable or out-of-date products or services.

- Entrance into new markets.
- New products and services in current markets.
- The distribution structure.
- The advertising program.
- The economic and pricing program.
- New product design and enhancements of current products.
- Service performance and quality standards.

Balancing objectives always requires a decision to take some risks. Management must weigh objectives in terms of the following:

1. Attainable profitability. What rate of return or margin of profit can you achieve now versus in the future?
2. Demands of immediate versus more distant future. What can you delay attaining in order to achieve more long-range objectives?
3. Other company objectives. What trade-offs can be made between desired performance in one area and desired performance in another?

You will need to decide, for example, which is more important, an expansion in markets and sales volume or a higher rate of return? How much time, effort, and energy should be expended on improving manufacturing productivity? Each company must decide on its own balance of future goals and short-term results.

All objectives should be set within the framework of your environmental analysis and the future product position you would like to achieve. As in other planning stages, make sure that all departments are involved in developing goals. Department heads should feel the plan is theirs; this attitude should help reduce conflicts and power struggles among departments when the marketing plan is to be implemented.

Assumptions Underlying Objectives

No set of objectives in a marketing plan should be presented without first stating the assumptions upon which they depend. *Assumptions* are estimates of future operating conditions for your marketing plan. You may not be able to predict exactly what is going to happen, but you must contend with a variety of possibilities as you implement your plan.

Stated assumptions explain in many instances why certain objectives were developed. Those who read your plan can judge whether or not the assumptions are valid or reasonable. Any disagreements over basic assumptions should be resolved at this stage to prevent more serious conflicts from erupting later, which could prove costly to the firm.

In the marketing plan, typical assumptions could be related to the following conditions:

- Changes in the Gross National Product (GNP).
- Anticipated inflation rate.
- Status and projected objectives of key competitors.
- Raw material availability and cost.
- Consumer disposable income.
- Anticipated interest rates.
- Government regulations.
- Expected new innovations.
- Market size.
- Competitor action.

When stating your assumptions, make sure (1) they are categorized and (2) they are stated as specifically as possible.

Categorizing Assumptions

When categorizing assumptions, it is not necessary to cover the entire range of conditions that may occur. Develop only those assumptions likely to influence the achievement of your objectives. For example, you could categorize assumptions about the economy and your competition as follows:

1. With respect to general economic conditions, we assume that
   - GNP will increase by 3.9 percent per year over the next three years.
   - The prime rate will rise from 8.7 percent to 9.6 percent over the next three years.
2. With respect to our competitors, we assume that
   - They will not differentiate their current product lines.
   - No new entrants are expected this year into the market.

Stating Assumptions Specifically

After you have categorized your assumptions, state them as specifically as you can. The degree to which you can quantify an assumption depends on the information available to you. You can define your assumptions according to three levels of specificity: general, specific, and quantified. For example:

1. General. The market for Product A will be up.

2. Specific. The market for Product A will be up 8 percent in the next twelve months.

3. Quantified. The market for Product A will increase at an 8 percent rate of growth because of an expected GNP of 3.9 percent and a 6.4 percent lower trade deficit.

The more information you have on hand, the more detailed your assumptions will be.

Developing assumptions is a critical step toward establishing your marketing objectives. You have a chance to identify factors that are somewhat unpredictable and uncontrollable and yet will affect the outcome of your objectives. These factors will become even more important after the plan is implemented and you begin monitoring your progress toward company objectives.

This stage is also a good time to develop contingency or "what if?" assumptions. What if your competition enters the market first? What if energy prices continue to fall? Develop alternative assumptions and objectives to the ones you put in your marketing plan. (Contingency objectives are discussed at the end of this chapter.) Once you have drawn up your list of assumptions, you must establish criteria for selecting and developing objectives.

Criteria for Objectives

Proactive planners use three primary criteria when developing sound objectives. They seek to establish objectives that are

- Measurable—to raise sales by a specific percentage, to increase production by a specific number of units.
- Realistic—based on a sound assessment of the company's resources and conditions in the marketplace.
- Attainable—objectives can be reasonably attained within the time frame stipulated.

In addition, you should strive to make your objectives results oriented, flexible, and acceptable to all departments in the company. While these criteria may seem somewhat idealistic, they are not as constraining as they look. Remember that objectives are broader in scope than either strategies or tactics. If your objectives satisfy most or all of the criteria, you will have a clear idea of the desired end results you are pursuing.

Using these criteria as a guide, ask yourself some basic questions when formulating your marketing objectives. For example:

- Is this a realistic and attainable objective?

- Is this objective consistent with the others we have developed?
- Are these objectives within our area of responsibility?
- Have we thoroughly assessed the needs and the wants of our consumers?
- Is the current market large enough to absorb the product quantity stated in our objectives?
- Can the firm's production facilities actually produce the product at a competitive price and in the estimated quantity?
- What reactions can we expect from competitors, and how will their reactions affect the achievement of our goal?
- How will attaining this objective affect other products, departments, and functions in the firm?
- Is the new venture we are proposing compatible with the company's long-term growth objectives?
- Are our products too far along in their product life cycle stage to obtain the desired profit margin?

Such criteria can be used to test your thinking before you select objectives and develop strategies to meet them. Be sure you have considered as many contingencies as possible and that your resulting objectives are based on sound research and analysis. Once you have completed this step, you are ready to formulate your marketing objectives.

Examples of Marketing Objectives

We developed sample objectives for each major marketing mix area. These lists are merely representative and cover only a few conditions for each area. You can adapt the lists to fit your company's particular situation.

Product-related Objectives

1. Differentiate products A and B back to their Growth Stage by the year 19__.
2. Reduce production expenses by 3 percent over the next twelve months.
3. Increase market penetration in area X by 7 percent during the next twelve months.
4. Expand into geographic location Y within the next nine months and obtain a 17 percent market share.

5. Study effects of dropping products that have a gross margin of 7 percent or less.

Price-related Objectives

1. Increase ROI by 1.6 percent for next fiscal year.
2. Decrease price of Product A by 4 percent to stimulate demand, assuming that Product A's price is elastic.
3. Decrease our average collection period from 62 days to 45 days by changing the current credit policy to 3/10/Net 30.
4. Prices should be competitive—within 7 percent of our major competitors—and yield a minimum unit contribution to profit of 12 percent.
5. Increase profitability of personal sales calls by use of telemarketing to screen uninterested customers, which will lower cost per sales call.
6. Change price of Product A to $x to compete directly in the high-income market segment.

Promotion Objectives

1. Increase buyer awareness of products A and B by x percent by December 31, 19__.
2. Develop high-quality inquiries at $x/inquiry for the company's products.
3. Decrease advertising in Cash Cow products by x percent and expend those dollars on products with a gross margin of 17 percent or better.

Distribution Objectives

1. Establish three new distributors in specific geographic regions by December 31, 19__.
2. Phase out all marginally profitable sales channels and centralize operations.

Other Objectives

You would also develop objectives for such areas as new venture development, budget and control, service programs, customer relations, profitability, market share, and any other areas that are essential for your firm. The more complete your list of objectives, the more clearly you will be able to monitor results as you implement your plan.

Contingency Objectives

Contingency objectives are one of the hallmarks of successful market planning. The internal and external environment for any firm is constantly changing. For example, a major competitor may merge with an industry giant who has cash to spare. They may lower prices below break-even to gain market share and drive out competitors. Your firm will need to act quickly in order to survive.

Proactive planning means that you consider several courses of action based on "what if?" questions. What if your major supplier experiences a labor strike that paralyzes production? What if distribution costs unexpectedly increase? What if someone tampers with your product?

Successful firms spend considerable time developing contingency objectives when they identify their basic assumptions. Should conditions call for them, contingency objectives then become the new marketing objectives.

Form 7: Marketing Objectives is designed to help you establish your strategic marketing objectives for the marketing mix and other functional areas such as training, sales, and production. By clarifying your objectives, you will be able to develop strategies to achieve them. A completed Form 7 is presented in the Sample Case.

Summary

- Marketing objectives are the core of the marketing plan. They are the link between the corporate level of planning and each department plan and provide targets for the direction and guidance of marketing strategies.

- Balancing near-term and longer-range objectives requires weighing objectives according to (1) attainable profitability, (2) demands of immediate versus more distant future, and (3) other competing objectives.

- No set of objectives should be presented without first stating the assumptions upon which they depend. Assumptions are estimates of future operating conditions for your marketing plan. They explain why certain objectives were developed rather than others.

- When stating assumptions, make sure they are categorized and stated as specifically as possible. You can define your assumptions according to three levels: general, specific, and quantified.

- Proactive planners seek to establish objectives that are measurable, realistic, and attainable.

- During this stage of strategic planning, you should also begin developing contingency objectives based on "what if?" questions.

Sample Case
Assumptions, Objectives, and the Future

Now that the marketing team had completed work on the firm's basis view, product positions, portfolio analysis, and problem and opportunity analysis, they had the data to develop a set of basic assumptions and establish overall corporate marketing objectives.

Although Haines preferred quantified assumptions, he realized that this time around many of the firm's assumptions would be general or only somewhat specific. Because it was the first year that the planning process had been conducted in the firm, some of the data were still rough or based on managers' estimates or best judgments. As the process was repeated in the future, the data would become more complete and quantitative.

However, if too many of the assumptions for a certain product line were general, Haines would know that firm data were lacking to support the objectives. His team could then focus on getting more information about that particular product line for next year's planning process.

The marketing team developed and categorized their basic assumptions. (These assumptions are abbreviated for purposes of the Sample Case. In actual fact, assumptions are often lengthy and more detailed.) The assumptions are as follows:

1. Economic conditions
   - The GNP will remain steady at 3.1 percent over the next three years.
   - Consumer Price Index will remain steady at 4.1 percent per year for the next two years and will increase to 5.3 percent by the end of the third year.
2. Competition
   - Direct foreign competition with our computer products will increase by 23 percent over the next three years.
   - Price cutting will continue for office products (non-computer) and stabilize in two years after the market is saturated.
   - The number of U.S. entrants into computer peripherals area is expected to increase 18 percent over the next eighteen months.
3. Raw materials
   - Certain microchips will be in short supply over the next twelve months until suppliers can expand their capacity.

- Prices of electronic components will drop by 24 percent due to increased foreign suppliers.

4. Government regulations
   - Import quotas will be imposed on foreign electronics firms over the next twenty-four months.

5. Market size
   - Market size is not expected to increase substantially for Product Lines 1, 2, and 6.
   - Market size for Product Line 4 is expected to decrease by 59 percent in two years because of product obsolescence.
   - Market size will increase an average of 14 percent for Product Lines 3, 5, and 7 over the next two to four years.

The marketing team was eager to begin setting corporate marketing objectives, but Haines reined in their enthusiasm.

"I want to be sure you understand the context for developing these objectives. First of all, they have to fulfill the requirements of the Business Plan and the Corporate Mission Statement. You all have copies of these documents? Good.

"Second, all objectives should be set within the framework of our environmental analysis and the future product positioning we want to achieve for each product.

"And third," Haines looked carefully around the table at each team member, "we have to involve all department heads and staff in developing these objectives."

An immediate chorus of protest erupted. "We can't do that," one team member said. "If we have to involve them in this step, the process will take forever!"

"Just getting them to meet with us will take a week," another member said.

"Have you ever tried talking with some of the product managers?" a third staff member demanded. "You can't get five minutes without an interruption."

Haines let the protests run on a little longer, then spoke up. "I'm going to say this over and over until everyone understands: The more we involve people in the planning process, the more ownership and investment in its success they'll have. Think about it. How would you feel if the production department set the objectives for the marketing team without consulting you?"

The team was silent.

"All right, how do you think the product managers are going to react when you present them with a finished plan, complete with objectives and strategies, that they had no part in developing?"

The team exchanged guilty glances.

"I'm a strong believer in a company where all employees are team players. It may be hard to work with at first, but in the long run it prevents a lot of conflicts and power struggles among people. What we're doing in this planning process is more than simply gathering data and analyzing questionnaires. We're building a team that involves everyone from top management down to support staff who will work together to achieve the company's goals."

Haines softened his approach. "Don't worry about getting time to meet with managers or anyone else you need to see. I'll arrange that with the partners."

Haines then gave the team some guidelines to use when working with department heads and staff on the objectives. "The criteria for all objectives are that they should be measurable, realistic, and attainable. They must be balanced in terms of attainable profitability, the demands of the immediate versus the long-term future, and other objectives the managers may have. Any questions?"

"Yes. Suppose we can't agree on a set of objectives? Who will arbitrate?"

"I'll be available to help resolve any disputes, and so will the three partners. Keep in mind that you have top management support for this process, not just my backing. All right, let's get started. I'll set up the first meetings by the end of this week, and we'll set a target date for the first of next month to have all the corporate objectives set."

By the end of the month, despite some difficulties working with management and their staffs, the team had finished their task. The overall abbreviated corporate marketing objectives follow.

I. Overall Corporate Marketing Objectives

- Increase ROI by an average 2.1 percent for the entire seven product lines over the next eighteen months.
- Decrease service complaints by 70 percent by the end of the current fiscal year.
- Establish sales and service training programs to train staff in characteristics of Product Line 7 (AutoDrive). Introduce telemarketing techniques in sales department.
- Decrease production costs by 4.8 percent through automation over the next twelve months.
- Extend collection period from thirty days to forty-five days to stimulate dealer orders.

II. Product Marketing Objectives—All Seven Lines

- Differentiate Product Line 1 back toward its Growth Stage in the next two years. If this is not feasible, R & D should develop replacement products to introduce in three years.

- Decrease advertising expense on Cash Cow Product Line 1 by 82 percent and channel those funds to the advertising budgets for Product Lines 2, 5, and 7 (Auto-Drive).
- Decrease price of Product Line 2 to meet competition's price and to minimize market share loss.
- Enhance features of Product Line 3 to appeal to new segments and to increase market share by 11 percent by the end of the third quarter.
- Drop Product Line 4 from the portfolio. Stop expending any additional funds to market these products.
- Expand Product Line 7 (AutoDrive) into the West Coast region through increased sales and service force; obtain a 12 percent market share within twelve months.
- Increase buyer awareness of Product Line 7 by 34 percent over the next twelve months.
- Open new channel of distribution through joint venture for Product Lines 5 and 7 within nine months.

Once the overall corporate marketing and product line objectives were set, the product managers' next step was to develop objectives for each line. Haines devised a form to help them set objectives for each of the marketing mix elements and any additional goals that might be required.

He focused particular attention on Line 7, AutoDrive, since the product's official entry into the national market was only a few months away. When the form was completed, Haines felt confident they had established a set of realistic objectives that would enable DataStar to achieve the greatest return from the product.

The next step for his marketing team was to work with management and other personnel to select the best strategies and contingency plans to achieve DataStar's new objectives.

Form 7   Marketing Objectives

Product: AutoDrive   Date: _____

I. Overall Corporate Marketing Objectives

List and describe overall marketing objectives:

(1) Increase ROI by an average 2.1 percent for the entire seven product lines over the next

eighteen months.

(2) Decrease service complaints by 70 percent by the end of the current fiscal year.

(3) Establish sales and service training programs to train staff in characteristics of Product Line

7 (AutoDrive) for national market. Introduce telemarketing techniques in sales department.

(4) Decrease production costs by 4.8 percent through automation over the next twelve months.

(5) Extend collection period from thirty days to forty-five days to stimulate dealer orders.

II. Product Marketing Objectives

List and describe marketing objectives for each major marketing criterion:

Profitability

(1) Minimum of 17 percent return on product investment over life of the product.

Pricing

(1) Position product to upper 15 percent of people willing to pay higher price; lower price to next level of price-sensitive buyers when segment is nearly saturated.

(2) Offer volume discounts up to 20 percent to high-volume distributors.

(3) Achieve ROI of 14 percent in first year and increase to 22 percent by end of third year.

Market Share

(1) Gain one-third of total market by end of third year.

(2) Gain 12 percent first year; increase to 24 percent by second year.

Promotion/Advertising

(1) Position product as a premium item to convince market to pay high price.

(2) Achieve maximum market coverage through promotional activities.

(3) Use rapid skimming strategy.

Distribution

(1) Establish national distribution system of franchised dealers through alliance or acquisition.

(2) Offer longer collection periods to induce dealers to carry larger stocks to have complete product line.

Product Development

(1) Migrate current national customers to new product while phasing out old product.

(2) Create customer view of product as high-quality, premier item.

Sales Volume

Increase sales volume by an average of 12 percent over the next three years.

Other (training, customer relations, service)

(1) Increase training of sales and repair personnel.

(2) Introduce telemarketing techniques.

(3) Decrease turnaround time for repairs by 30 percent.

CHAPTER SEVEN

Choosing
Your Marketing Strategy

Introduction

Marketing strategies begin the action part of your marketing plan—how to get the job done. While objectives establish desired end results, strategies outline the specific marketing approaches needed to achieve those results.

The strategies you select should take into account the life cycle stage of your products; the marketing mix of product, price, promotion, and distribution; and such concerns as customer service and packaging. The creative implementation of these strategies will determine the effectiveness of your marketing plan.

At the same time, you should consider alternative strategies and outline contingency plans for achieving your objectives. Every proactive marketing plan contains provisions for the unexpected. If circumstances change radically or your primary plan proves ineffective, you will have contingency strategies on which to base an alternative plan. This practice will give you added flexibility in responding to changes in market conditions.

In this chapter, we provide a brief survey of product life cycle and product mix strategies, then discuss several other strategies—market segmentation and market niche, product differentiation, and product regeneration—in the final sections.

Because each firm's circumstances are unique, we can give only general guidelines about which strategy may be appropriate for you. However, one way to select the best strategy is to look at the current position of your products or services and their projected positions as analyzed in Chapters 3 and 4. Products in the Introduction, Growth, Mature, and Decline stages of their life cycle will all require different strategies to manage them. The more you know about each product's performance within its life cycle and the impact of that product on your portfolio, the better your chance of choosing the optimum strategy for your firm.

Marketing Strategy

Although definitions for the term vary, we define *marketing strategy* as a consistent, appropriate, and feasible set of principles through which a particular company hopes to achieve its long-run customer and profit objectives in a particular competitive environment.

Factors in Marketing Strategy

Whatever strategy you ultimately choose must take into account several factors:

- The company's position in the market.
- The company's mission, policies, objectives, and resources.
- Your competitors' marketing strategies.
- Buying behaviors of customers in your target markets.
- Your products' current and projected life cycle stage.
- General economic conditions in which you must do business.

The attainment of your objectives is the sole purpose of each strategic program. Each strategy must be linked to an objective, since any objective without a supporting strategy will not be accomplished. For example, if your objective is to increase Product A's market share by 14 percent, your strategy might outline how to reposition the product, reach a greater number of buyers within the market segment, and overhaul its pricing structure.

Requirements for Marketing Strategies

Each strategy you develop must meet four requirements:

1. It must meet specific deadlines. (When is the objective to be accomplished?)
2. It must control performance. (Are the proper steps being taken to achieve the objective?)
3. It must allocate resources directly and indirectly. (Do you have sufficient resources to accomplish your objective?)
4. It must be carefully timed. (Have you taken seasonal factors, economic conditions, etc. into account?)

Figure 7.1 Characteristics of Product Life Cycle Stages

Marketing Elements	Introduction Stage	Growth Stage	Mature Stage	Decline Stage
Sales	Low	Fast increases	Little or no growth	Decline
Cash Flow	Low to negative	Moderate	High	Low
Profits	Low to negative	Growing fast	Peak and decline	Very low
Competition	Little competition	Increasing in number and strength	Highly competitive	Declining in number
Customers/ Buyers	Early adopters/ innovators/risk takers	Mass market/ target market	Mass market/ replacement/ laggers	Replacement/ laggers
Marketing Expenditures	High	Continued high but decreasing as a percent of total sales	Declining	Very low

As you finalize your strategies, they must be fully communicated to everyone who will be involved in carrying them out. Successful implementation depends on the coordinated efforts of all concerned.

Product Life Cycle Strategies

As we discussed in Chapter 3, products go through a life cycle from their introduction into the market to their final demise. The four stages in the life cycle and their impact on various marketing elements are summarized in Figure 7.1.

Product life cycle strategies have been developed for each life cycle stage and for each of the four marketing elements: product, price, promotion, and distribution. These strategies have been implemented successfully by a wide range of firms from small, entrepreneurial companies to major corporations. To use these strategies effectively, you will need to know the life cycle stage for each of your products—information you developed in Chapter 3. We recommend that you consider life cycle strategies before evaluating the other strategies discussed in the next sections.

Strategies Matrix

Since there are a variety of situations and constraints that firms face in projecting product growth, it is not possible to list all the life cycle strategy combinations that could be developed. As a result, in Figure 7.2 we have put together a matrix of representative strategies for each life cycle stage and marketing mix element.

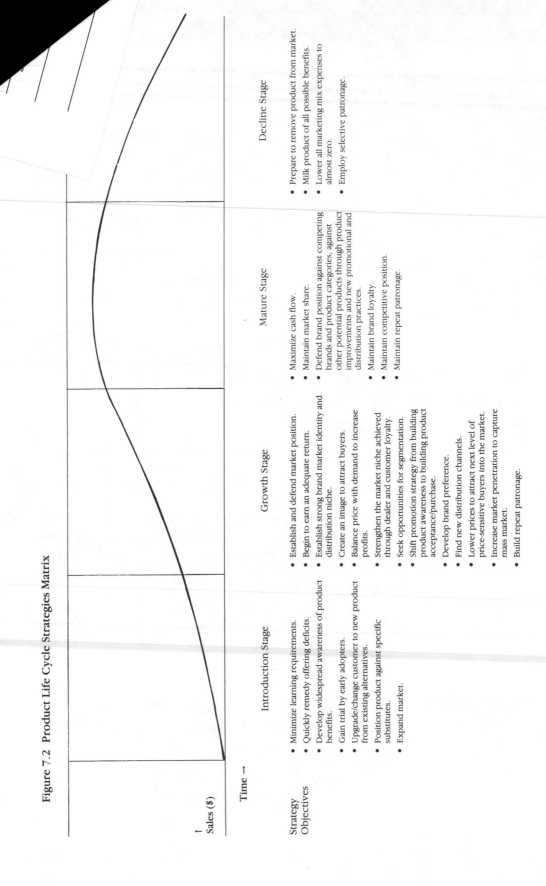

Figure 7.2 Product Life Cycle Strategies Matrix

Sales ($)

Time →

	Introduction Stage	Growth Stage	Mature Stage	Decline Stage
Strategy Objectives	• Minimize learning requirements. • Quickly remedy offering deficits. • Develop widespread awareness of product benefits. • Gain trial by early adopters. • Upgrade/change customer to new product from existing alternatives. • Position product against specific substitutes. • Expand market.	• Establish and defend market position. • Begin to earn an adequate return. • Establish strong brand market identity and distribution niche. • Create an image to attract buyers. • Balance price with demand to increase profits. • Strengthen the market niche achieved through dealer and customer loyalty. • Seek opportunities for segmentation. • Shift promotion strategy from building product awareness to building product acceptance/purchase. • Develop brand preference. • Find new distribution channels. • Lower prices to attract next level of price-sensitive buyers into the market. • Increase market penetration to capture mass market. • Build repeat patronage.	• Maximize cash flow. • Maintain market share. • Defend brand position against competing brands and product categories, against other potential products through product improvements and new promotional and distribution practices. • Maintain brand loyalty. • Maintain competitive position. • Maintain repeat patronage.	• Prepare to remove product from market. • Milk product of all possible benefits. • Lower all marketing mix expenses to almost zero. • Employ selective patronage.

Product Strategy	• Limited number of models. • Physical product and offering designs both focused on minimizing learning requirements. • Build association of brand name with product. • Product design and cost tailored to appeal to most receptive segment. • High attention to quality control. • Quick elimination of market-revealed defects in design. • Define product weaknesses.	• Maximize product quality. • Fit buyers' needs with product changes as needed. • Modular design to facilitate adding new features that appeal to different segments. • Eliminate unnecessary specialties with little market appeal. • Increase features.	• Pay close attention to possibilities for minor product improvement and cost cutting. • Pay close attention to opportunities through either bold cost and price penetration of new markets or through major product changes. • Consider introduction of new products.	• Eliminate any items not returning a direct profit.
Price Strategy	• Set high to cover initial costs. • Establish pricing to impose the minimum value perception learning and to match the value reference perception of the most receptive segment. • Use high trade discounts.	• Use trade discounts. • Have different prices from low end to premium product. • Use aggressive promotional pricing, with prices cut as fast as costs decline as the result of accumulated production experience. • Intensify sampling. • Increase attraction to market-broadening and promotional pricing opportunities.	• Use defensive pricing to maintain market share and product category franchise. • Search for incremental pricing opportunities. • Increase private label contracts to boost volume and gain an experience advantage. • Reposition price whenever demand patterns and competitors' strategies permit.	• Decline to increase remaining volume. • Maintain or decline profit level pricing with total disregard of any offsets on market share.
Promotion Strategy	• Create widespread awareness and understanding of benefits. • Gain trial by early adopters. • Use publicity, personal sales, mass media. • Aim at needs and wants of innovators.	• Create and strengthen brand preference among trade and final users. • Stimulate general trial. • Use mass media, personal sales, sampling, publicity, dealer promotions. • Make mass market aware of products and services.	• Maintain consumer and trade loyalty. • Put strong emphasis on dealers and distributors. • Promote more frequent use. Use mass media, dealer-oriented promotions. • Use promotion to differentiate among major competitors.	• Phase out promotion of product. • Keep only enough to maintain profitable distribution. • Emphaize low price to increase volume.
Distribution Strategy	• Use exclusive or selective strategy. • Have distributor margins high enough to justify heavy promotional spending. • Acquire high quality of distribution.	• Find new distribution channels. • Put strong emphasis on keeping dealer well supplied with minimum inventory cost. • Pay close attention to rapid resupply of distributor stocks.	• Strongly emphasize keeping dealers well supplied but at minimum inventory cost.	• Phase out outlets as they become marginalized.

At this point we are not concerned with developing specific tactical budgets and plans but with establishing an overall strategic approach for your firm. Each firm will have its own methods of determining such tactical actions as budgets for promotion and advertising. As you study the matrix, you may wish to note for yourself which strategies seem appropriate for your marketing plan.

Price/Promotion Life Cycle Strategies

Four price/promotion life cycle strategies are not included in Figure 7.2 because they need more detailed explanation. The approach is based on the strong relationship between price and promotion and may work well for your firm.

Introduction Stage. In the Introduction Stage of a new product, the market managers can set high or low levels of expenditures for all marketing mix variables. Since there is a strong relationship between the price and the promotion expenditures, the two can be used to set pricing strategies based on the promotional expenditures and mix. Four possible strategic alternatives are depicted in Figure 7.3.*

A *rapid skimming strategy* features a high price and high promotional effort to recover as much gross profit per unit as possible and to convince the market through promotional efforts that the product merits the high price. Thus, high promotion is expected to accelerate the rate of market penetration. The following assumptions must apply for this strategy to be successful:

- The majority of potential customers are initially unaware of the product.
- Customers who become aware of the product want it and will pay the high price to get it.
- The firm anticipates future competition and seeks to build early brand preference and loyalty.

A *slow skimming strategy* uses high price and low promotion activities. The high price allows the maximum recovery of gross profit per unit while low promotion keeps expenses down. With this strategy, a firm seeks to skim high profits from the market. These assumptions apply to this strategy:

- Most customers are aware of the product.

---

*This section is based on Philip Kotler's discussion in *Marketing Management,* 5th ed. (Englewood Cliffs, N.J.: Prentice-Hall, 1984):363–64.

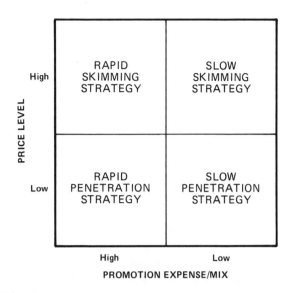

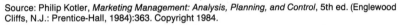

Figure 7.3   Skimming/Penetration Strategy

Source: Philip Kotler, *Marketing Management: Analysis, Planning, and Control*, 5th ed. (Englewood Cliffs, N.J.: Prentice-Hall, 1984):363. Copyright 1984.

- Consumers who want the product will pay the high price.
- The threat of potential competition is low.
- The potential market is small.

A *rapid penetration strategy* uses low price and heavy promotion. This strategy will result in the fastest market penetration and largest market share for the company. For this strategy to be successful, the following assumptions must apply:

- Economies of scale for the manufacturing process exist.
- Buyers are price sensitive.
- There is strong potential competition.
- Customers are relatively unaware of the product.
- The market is large.

A *slow penetration strategy* features low price and low promotion. Low prices will increase the market's acceptance of the product. Low promotional expenses mean greater profits on product sales. This strategy is based on the following assumptions:

- A large market exists.
- There is some potential competition.

- Customers are highly aware of the product.
- The market is price sensitive.

Growth Stage. The Growth Stage, which will result from the Introduction Stage strategies, may require some adjustments in those strategies to keep the product competitive and profitable. Remember in using product life cycle strategies to select the strategies that correlate to your product's stage. Otherwise your strategies will not be compatible with your product and its environment, and will not lead to the fulfillment of your objectives.

Mature Stage. Strategies for the Mature Stage include market modification, product differentiation, and product regeneration.

Market Modification Strategy. This strategy focuses on looking for opportunities to find new buyers for the product. These opportunities can include identifying new markets and new segments and increasing product usage among current customers.

Product Differentiation Strategy. This strategy seeks to attract new customers or increase current customers' usage by changing the product in some way.

Product Regeneration Strategy. This strategy attempts to extend the life cycle of a product by finding new uses for it and repositioning it back to the Growth Stage.

Decline Stage. When a product enters the Decline Stage, it must be managed by exploring a variety of strategic alternatives. Since each of the possible strategies has a different purpose, the marketing mix possibilities for each one can vary widely. Thus, the marketing mix selection depends not only on the strategy chosen, but also on the environmental conditions in which the product operates.

Because of this factor, we have omitted marketing mix alternatives from our discussion of Decline Stage strategies. These alternatives will have to be formulated by the product manager according to each product's specific situation. These are the strategic alternatives:

Continuation Strategy. Under this strategy, you continue to market the product in its present segments using current pricing, distribution, and promotion programs until you decide to drop the product from the portfolio.

Product Maintenance Strategy. With this strategy, you do not sell the product to new customers because superior products have already filled its market niche. Instead, you offer only maintenance parts and systems to current customers until a new substitute product fills the void.

Product Modification Strategy. Because in the Decline Stage much of the market has shifted to substitute products, this strategy will be more difficult to apply. It should be used only if your product has some minor defect that can be easily identified and changed. You should not commit any sizable amount of funds to product modifications unless market research clearly shows that the new product will be a strong competitor in a new market.

If this strategy was not implemented during the Mature Stage of a product's life cycle, the Decline Stage represents the last opportunity to use it. Proceed cautiously, however.

Concentration Strategy. Under this strategy, you concentrate your resources only on the strongest markets and channels while phasing out the product everywhere else.

Phase-out Strategy. You can take advantage of declining demand by phasing out the product gradually, since it may still contribute to company objectives or have some impact on sales or support other products. You gradually decrease expenditures on the product and discontinue maintenance parts and systems, and so on.

In using this strategy, you must assess the impact of phasing out the product on other offerings in the company portfolio. If market research shows it is economical to continue offering the product despite its low or negative cash flow, you can use the phase-out strategy until a substitute product is developed.

Product Elimination Strategy. In this strategy, you increase a product's current profits by sharply reducing all expenses associated with its marketing program. This approach accelerates the rate of sales decline and quickly eliminates the product from the market.

Market Segmentation

Market segmentation is a fairly recent advance in marketing strategy. It begins not with identifying product possibilities but with determining customer groups and their needs.

The power of this concept is easily apparent. In any environment intensely competitive for the customer dollar, a firm can prosper by developing products and services for specific market segments. A company can target particular groups rather than blanket the entire market, and it can achieve a higher rate of return for the dollars it has invested.

The question is how to identify and categorize the market and what criteria to use for developing segments within it.

Identifying and Categorizing the Market

For market segmentation to be effective, two general conditions must be met.

First, you must identify and categorize actual or potential customers into relatively homogeneous segments according to their responses to marketing mix variables.

Second, you must be able to identify characteristics of these segments or groups that can be used as a basis for special marketing efforts to reach them.

A practical approach for identifying and categorizing differences and preferences among customers is to ask the following questions.

Who

- are the members of segments that have been identified through the previous questions?
- buys our product or service?
- buys our competitors' products or services?

What

- benefits do customers seek?
- factors influence demand?
- function does the product perform for the customer?
- are important buying criteria?
- is the basis of comparison with other products?
- risks does the customer perceive?

How

- do customers buy?
- long does the buying process last?
- do customers use the product?
- does the product fit into their life-styles or operations?
- much are they willing to spend?
- much do they buy?

Where

- is the decision made to buy?
- do customers seek information about products or services?
- do customers buy the product or service?

When

- is the first decision to buy made?
- is the product repurchased?

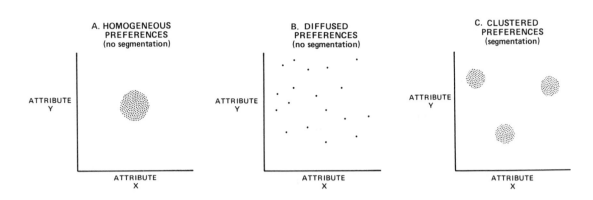

Figure 7.4 Customer Preferences and Market Segmentation

Answers to these questions can help you to identify customer segments by categorizing their preferences. Figure 7.4 summarizes these categories as homogeneous, diffused, and clustered.

In some markets, customers' preferences will be *homogeneous*, that is, they will prefer the same characteristics in a product or service. For example, if the product is a dirt bike, they may all prefer heavy tires, foot brakes, and a lightweight frame. In this case there is only one segment, and no market segmentation can occur.

In other markets, preferences will be *diffused*. There will be no clear-cut desires for various product or service characteristics. Suppose, for example, that everyone wanted a different type of dirt bike: some with hand brakes, others with 24-inch wheels, still others with 16-inch wheels, some with a heavy frame, and others with a light one. Since no concentration exists, there are a multitude of smaller markets. Again, segmentation cannot occur.

In the third market, customer preferences are *clustered* around various product or service characteristics. In our example above, one group of customers wants a dirt bike with hand brakes, lighter wheels, and a heavier frame; another group wants foot brakes, dropped handlebars, and heavier wheels; and still another group wants foot brakes, raised handlebars, and a lightweight frame. These clusters of customer preferences identify natural market segments. You would then be able to develop marketing strategies to target the needs of these segments.

Segmenting Markets—Five Variables

Once you have identified the market and determined that it can be segmented, you can use five variables as the basis for grouping consumers into target segments. These variables include segmentation according to behavioristic, geographic, demographic, pyschographic, and benefit factors.

Behavioristic segmentation focuses on customers' behavior in the market. Many marketers believe that behavioristic variables are the starting point in identifying segments. Behavior can be categorized in several ways:

- Purchase occasion—customers who share a similar occasion (anniversary, birthday) for purchasing a product or service.

- Benefits sought—customers' motivations for purchasing the product or service.

- Use status—customers who can be grouped as nonusers, users, first-time users, and regular users.

- Usage rate—customers who can be grouped as light, medium, or heavy users of a product or service.

- Loyalty status—how loyal various customers are to a company's particular product or service.

Geographic segmentation groups customers according to some geographic feature such as region, county, city, population density, or climate. This method is easy to apply and useful for many products, particularly where distribution is a key factor.

Demographic segmentation permits the marketing strategist to classify purchases in a direct and efficient manner. Demographic variables include sex, family size, age, race, and income. Relating buying patterns to one or more of these variables is useful in targeting the segment.

Psychographic segmentation focuses on such variables as personality traits, life-style, and buyer motives to segment a market. Such information can increase a firm's understanding of buyer behavior, although data may be difficult to obtain. From a marketing perspective, psychographic information is useful in diagnosing markets and in deciding what action to take.

Psychographic data may be particularly helpful in the beginning stages of developing marketing strategy because it can be used to determine why consumers buy. These data can then be correlated with demographic and geographic variables to fine-tune the strategy for a particular target market.

Benefit segmentation focuses on benefits associated with a product or service. It is used to determine what benefits or problems exist and their importance in a purchase decision. Benefits may be related to such factors as economics, social status, convenience, savings, and performance.

Criteria for Effective Segmentation

Once you have chosen the method to segment your market, you need to make sure the segment is worth the time and effort it will take to market your products. Effective segments should have the following characteristics:

- They must be substantial. Segments should be large enough and profitable enough to be worth a separate marketing effort.
- They must be measurable. You should be able to measure the size and purchasing power of the segments. Minimum cutoff points can be established for segment size and buying power. If the number of consumers within a segment falls below this cutoff point, the segment can either be combined with other segments or dropped.
- They must be accessible. You must be able to reach the segments through advertising and promotion, and you must be able to serve customers once you have reached them. Without accessibility, segmentation has little value.

Benefits of Segmentation

Given the limited resources of any firm, large or small, targeting specific segments offers three major benefits.

First, your firm is in a better position to spot and compare market opportunities. Customers may be dissatisfied with current suppliers and on the lookout for better products and services from another firm. Or changes in customer demand may present new opportunities you can exploit.

Second, your firm can develop marketing programs based on a clearer idea of how customers in specific segments will respond. You can focus your marketing efforts on segments most likely to purchase your products or services.

Third, you can make finer adjustments in your products or services and marketing programs. You can tailor your offerings and programs to the needs of each segment and respond more quickly to changes in customer requirements.

Segmenting and targeting markets can enable you to satisfy customer needs, capture a higher return on investment, and increase profitability.

Market Niche Strategy

Market niche strategy is based on segmentation and can be used in conjunction with a market segmentation strategy. Many companies use a niche strategy to avoid direct competition with market leaders in an industry. Instead, these companies identify and serve a specific segment or market niche of a larger market. Firms can specialize in developing products and services for these niches, which are usually ignored or overlooked by the market leaders.

Niche strategies are being used by all sizes of firms across many industries. In fact, market niching is becoming the primary strategy of many successful firms. Most of these firms compete in areas where their particular strengths are highly valued; they specialize rather than diversify; and they emphasize profits over sales growth or market share.

The key to market niche strategy is *specialization*. A company may specialize in the types of end users it services or in a particular customer group or geographic region. It may provide special products, services, quality features, or pricing structures. Whatever form specialization takes, it is essential to a firm's success.

When identifying market niches, you should look for the following characteristics:

- The niche is large with enough purchasing power to yield a profit.
- The niche has been overlooked or ignored by the market leader.
- The niche can be serviced efficiently and effectively by your company.
- The niche can be defended against the market leader and other competitors by using the goodwill you develop with customers.

Your major goal in using this strategy is to find specific market segments that your firm can serve to the best of its ability.

Product Differentiation

Product differentiation is defined as changes in a product's characteristics that will attract new customers or increase usage among current customers. These changes include quality, feature, and style improvements. It is important to recognize, however, that product variations are not based on an analysis of natural market segments. Product differentiation is used to hold or capture more of a market that has already been defined and penetrated.

One of the best examples of product differentiation strategy can be seen in the famous "burger wars" among the top fast-food chains. McDonald's, Wendy's, and Burger King all sought to differentiate a basic product—the hamburger—in order to increase their share of the highly competitive fast-food market. Thus, consumers were treated to the flame-broiled hamburger, the gourmet burger, and the have-it-your-way burger.

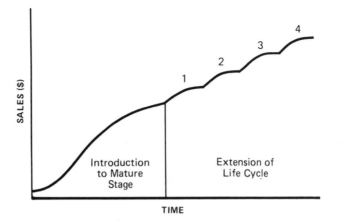

Figure 7.5   Product Regeneration

Product differentiation is a particularly important concept when a product reaches its Mature Stage. Competition intensifies, prices drop, and sellers' earnings decline. At this stage, companies recognize the value of introducing different product features, quality, or style as a way of maintaining or capturing customer attention and loyalty. This approach leads to a proliferation of sizes, models, options, packaging, discounts, and other variations for a product that is essentially the same among competitors.

Product Regeneration

In the late Mature Stage of a product, dollar sales have peaked and begun to decline. Firms can use *product regeneration* to extend the life cycle of a product by finding new uses, new markets, new product characteristics, or updating the basic product. This approach repositions the product to its Growth Stage, as shown in Figure 7.5.

If product regeneration is not feasible, the product will continue to fall into the Decline Stage and eventually be dropped from the company's portfolio.

Developing Contingency Strategies

Just as contingency objectives are needed in any successful market plan, so are contingency strategies. At some point, changes inside or outside the firm may prevent you from achieving your original goals. You will need to have an alternative course of action to fall back on. Also, developing contingency strategies will ensure that you have looked at several alternative plans and given yourself the opportunity to choose the best one. You will be in a better position to counter your competitors' strategies as they change.

Contingency strategies need not be given in detail in your marketing plan. In fact, doing so may interfere with the smooth implementation of the strategies you select as your primary action program. You need give only a brief statement covering your contingency strategies and your readiness to implement them if necessary.

Evaluating Primary Strategies Selected

Once you have chosen the primary strategies to meet your company's objectives, evaluate these strategies for possible self-defeating conflicts before you set them in final form. The basic criteria for evaluation include the following:

- Internal compatibility. Is the specific strategy or strategies you have chosen compatible with the assigned objective?
- External compatibility. Is the strategy compatible with external market conditions?
- Resource availability. Are all the resources you need to accomplish the strategy available?
- Time frame. Are the strategy deadlines compatible with the time frame outlined in the objective? Do you have enough time to complete the steps called for in the strategy? Have you mapped out the sequence and timing of various marketing efforts that will need to be implemented?
- Risk factor. How much of your total resources are committed to this strategy? If you begin to vary from the strategy significantly or if the strategy fails, will this mean failure to achieve the objective? Keep in mind that the risk of failure increases as the time allotted to a specific strategy is extended.

Evaluating your selected strategies can help you spot weaknesses or contradictions before you implement your plan.

Form 8: Marketing Strategies contains a separate sheet for each of the marketing mix elements. The form can help you to clarify your strategies and to formulate contingency plans should your original strategies prove inadequate in the face of changing market conditions. The completed Form 8 for the Sample Case will give you some idea of the contingencies you may want to consider.

Summary

- Marketing strategy is a consistent, appropriate, and feasible set of principles through which a particular company hopes to achieve its long-run customer and profit objectives in a particular competitive environment. Strategies should take into account the life cycle stage of your products, the marketing mix, and such concerns as customer service and packaging.

- The sole purpose of each strategic program is attaining company objectives. Each strategy must be linked to an objective and must (1) meet specific deadlines, (2) control performance, (3) allocate resources directly and indirectly, and (4) be carefully timed.

- Product life cycle strategies are developed according to the life cycle stage of each product.

- Price/promotion life cycle strategies are based on a potentially strong relationship between price and promotion. In the Introduction Stage, four strategic alternatives are rapid skimming, slow skimming, rapid penetration, and slow penetration.

- Mature Stage strategies include market modification, product differentiation, and product regeneration.

- Decline Stage strategies include continuation, product maintenance, product modification, concentration, phase-out, and product elimination.

- Market segmentation is based on identifying customer groups and their needs. A firm must identify and categorize customers into relatively homogeneous segments and identify characteristics of these segments that can be used as a basis for special marketing efforts.

- Markets can be segmented on the basis of behavioristic, geographic, demographic, psychographic, or benefit characteristics. To be useful, segments must be substantial, measurable, and accessible.

- Market niche strategy is based on segmentation and is used to identify and serve a specific segment of a larger market. The key to market niche strategy is specialization to avoid direct competition with market leaders.

- Product differentiation is defined as changes in a product's characteristics that will attract new customers or increase usage among current customers. This strategy is used to hold or capture a market already defined and penetrated.

- Product regeneration can extend the life cycle of a product by finding new uses, new markets, or new product characteristics, or by updating the product.

- Contingency strategies are an important part of your marketing plan. They will ensure that you have an alternative course of action to fall back on to counter competitors' strategies.

- Once you have chosen your primary strategies, evaluate them for internal and external compatibility, resource availability, appropriate time frame, and risk factor.

Sample Case   New Strategy for Success

When it came time to select the best strategies for DataStar, Haines made sure that his marketing team and all department heads and their staffs understood two important points.

"First, remember that the marketing strategies we choose for the firm serve as the objectives for each product plan. Second, always keep the portfolio view in mind. Product managers are not developing their plans in a vacuum. They must take into account the strategies for other products as well.

"Say, for example, we're putting too much money into a Cash Cow item. The strategy to lower expenditures for that product must be coordinated with a strategy to raise expenditures for other products that need an infusion of cash. Strategy development is a very interactive process; that's a key point I want you to remember."

Haines explained that the marketing team and top management would work on selecting the overall strategy to achieve the firm's objectives. Department heads and product managers would then develop their own strategic plans based on the company's overall marketing strategy. He gave the team and all management-level personnel some guidelines for selecting their strategies.

"Be sure to take into account the company's position in the market; our mission, policies, objectives, and resources; our knowledge of the competitors' strategies; the buying behaviors of our target customers; our products' current and projected life cycle stages; and the general economic conditions in which we do business.

"*The attainment of objectives is the sole purpose of each strategic program*. You must have a strategy linked to each objective. The strategy you develop must satisfy four criteria: it must meet specific deadlines, control performance, allocate resources directly and indirectly, and be carefully timed.

"We'll develop the corporate marketing strategy first and then help each department and product manager develop their own strategies. In my experience, it takes about a month to get the job done."

Haines and his team met with Price, Koster, and Simic to choose the corporate strategy. After a week of discussion, they selected a life cycle strategy for each product. The marketing team devised a matrix outlining general strategies for each of the four phases of a product's life cycle. The matrix was circulated to all department heads and product managers. The marketing team helped them to coordinate their strategies in light of the firm's portfolio view.

When all department and product plans were completed, the managers turned them into the marketing department. All strategies were evaluated by the marketing team for internal and external compatibility, resource availability, appropriate time frames, and risk factor.

The sample Form 8 has been completed for AutoDrive and shows the development of individual product strategies. Each strategy has a contingency plan that can be put into effect should the primary strategy fail.

Form 8   Marketing Strategies

Product: _____AutoDrive_____   Date: _____

I. Product Objectives and Strategies

1. Describe product objectives:

(1) Migrate current customers to new product while phasing out old product over next six

to seven months.

(2) Create customer perception of product as high quality, premier item.

2. Describe product strategies:

(1) Designed and engineered to appeal to most receptive segment; produced in modular

fashion for easy add-ons and future enhancements.

(2) High attention to quality control.

(3) Quick elimination of defects revealed in the market.

3. Describe briefly contingency strategies and under what conditions they would be implemented:

If competition offers equal product, DataStar will stress its product's quality, superior

engineering, and strong customer support and service. We will also differentiate product by

enhancing current stand-alone features bought separately with single unit. Easy to do because

of modular design.

II. Pricing Objectives and Strategies

1. Describe pricing objectives for the product:

(1) Position product toward upper 15 percent of people willing to pay higher price for this type of item.

(2) Offer volume discounts of maximum 20 percent to distributors.

(3) Achieve ROI of 14 percent first year and increase to 22 percent at end of third year.

2. Describe pricing strategies for the product:

(1) Use a rapid skimming strategy to increase market share so that economies of scale will result in higher profit margins in later years.

(2) Offer higher dealer volume discounts to keep distributor channels open.

(3) Use pricing strategy of going to next level of price-sensitive buyers when market segment is almost saturated.

3. Describe briefly contingency strategies and under what conditions they would be implemented:

If market becomes crowded with many competitors, shift pricing policy to match competitors' prices. This will allow the firm to maintain and increase market share. In general, the technology is changing so rapidly that product may be in the Mature Stage in two years instead of projected three years; therefore, the firm will have to shift to Mature Stage strategies. This condition would affect all strategies for this product.

III. Promotion/Advertising Objectives and Strategies

1. Describe promotion/advertising objectives for product:

(1) Position product as premier to convince market to pay the higher price.

(2) Maximize market coverage.

(3) Use rapid skimming strategy.

2. Describe promotion/advertising strategies for product:

(1) Create and strengthen brand preference among trade and private users.

(2) Use select mass media, personal sales, and dealer promotions.

(3) Make mass market aware of products and services.

(4) Have special promotion to reach volume customers.

(5) Tie current product in as new replacement for an old product to attract new users and migrate old users to the new product.

3. Describe briefly contingency strategies and under what conditions they would be implemented:

If competition increases, emphasize product differentiation strategy, focusing on product features, company reputation and services, and defensive advertising.

IV. Distribution Objectives and Strategies

1. Describe distribution objectives for product:

(1) National distribution system of franchised dealers.

(2) Offer longer collection periods to induce dealers to carry larger stock and to have complete product line.

2. Describe distribution strategies for product:

(1) Locate high-quality distribution channels.

(2) Set production schedule so that dealers have minimum backlog of orders.

(3) Schedule product demonstrations for dealers.

3. Describe briefly contingency strategies and under what conditions they would be implemented:

(1) Have alternative distribution channels available if competition increases and begins to saturate dealer channels.

(2) Offer dealers higher discounts to induce them to carry DataStar lines.

V. Other Objectives and Strategies

1. Describe other objectives for product:

At this stage none.

2. Describe other strategies for product:

At this stage none.

3. Describe briefly contingency strategies and under what conditions they would be implemented:

At this stage none.

CHAPTER EIGHT

Budget and Forecasting

Introduction

The marketing budget is directly related to the developed goals, strategies, and planned tactical actions of the marketing plan. While strategies outline your plan of attack, the budget specifies how much it will cost.

It is important to remember that drawing up a budget is not the same as strategic planning. Budgets provide control, monitor expenses, track revenue, and so on. If budgeting is used for overall planning or is the main focus of a plan, then the company's primary objectives may well shift to saving money rather than to generating a profit through long-range strategic planning.

As a result, we do not go into detail about how to prepare a budget. Each company has its own methods and procedures for accomplishing that task. Instead we present general guidelines on *how budgets fit into strategic planning and how they affect the success of a marketing plan.* Once overall budget requirements are approved at the strategic level, detailed budget figures can be taken care of at the tactical level.

Our approach follows up on the product/portfolio analyses discussed in Chapters 3 and 4, particularly when we examine a product's contribution margin later in this chapter.

Organization of the Budget

The first step in developing a budget at the strategic level is to identify your own department's area of fiscal responsibility. Total marketing costs in many companies are the sum of all costs required to manufacture the product and put it into the hands of the customer. Many of these costs may be for functions or activities that are not necessarily part of your marketing plan or in your area of responsibility. Nevertheless, they must fit into the total allocation of resources available for marketing.

To isolate your area of responsibility, you will need to look at two broad categories of total marketing costs:

1. Order-getting costs—selling, advertising, promotion, incentives, packaging, and the like.

2. Order-filling costs—shipping, warehousing, inventory, order processing, billing, and so on.

Your marketing plan, including the objectives and strategies, is almost entirely concerned with the order-getting process. Creative deployment of the marketing mix aims at getting orders from customers. In addition, order-filling costs tend to be more fixed; the marketing manager has less control over these items than over order-getting costs. The more control you can exert over the costs associated with your department, the more favorable contribution to company profits your area can make.

The next step is to obtain budget estimates from each department in the firm associated with marketing activities. One person from each department should be responsible for providing budget information to the marketing department. Organize the budget into discrete categories, preferably by marketing function responsibility:

- Sales.
- Market research.
- Advertising.
- Production.
- Personnel (salaries and benefits).
- Other.

This approach makes it easier to agree on the measures and procedures that need to be followed to control expenses.

Make sure your budget format is compatible with the reporting procedures used in the accounting department. More corporations are using management information systems for control reporting and information purposes to help managers make decisions. If your format is compatible with these systems, it will be easier to obtain meaningful financial reports to help you control costs and manage your area of responsibility.

Budget and Forecasting

The marketing department is responsible for preparing a budget statement that reflects projected costs associated with the developed marketing plan as well as a revenue/sales forecast. This information is needed in order to implement the plan successfully. Budgets are developed at the corporate and individual product level.

Profit and Loss Statements

A simplified *corporate* budget statement, shown in Figure 8.1, is essentially a projected profit and loss (P and L) statement or a summation of all individual product sales and expenses.

The *individual product* budget statement is developed at the marketing department level and is illustrated in Figure 8.2, which shows a three-product profit and loss statement. The amount of detail included in a product-by-product P and L statement is up to the marketing department. Eventually all products are summed into a detailed pro forma P and L statement.

Forecasting

Forecasting is a way of predicting product demand and sales performance in the coming year or for a number of years. Once the product

Figure 8.1   A Simplified Profit and Loss Statement

Revenues from sales			$190,000
Cost of goods sold			80,000
Gross Margin			$110,000
Operating Expenses			
Selling Expenses			
Advertising expense	$10,000		
Marketing research expense	7,000		
Salary expense	35,000		
Miscellaneous expense	2,000		
Total Selling Expense		$54,000	
General/Administrative Expenses			
Rent expense	$11,000		
Insurance expense	4,000		
Supplies expense	3,000		
Depreciation expense	6,000		
Total G and A Expenses		$24,000	
Total Operating Expenses			$ 78,000
Net Profit (Loss) before Taxes			$ 32,000

Figure 8.2 Combined P and L Statement for Three Products

	Hardware	CRTs	Hard Disk Drive
Sales	$140,000	$35,000	$90,000
Cost of goods sold	58,000	17,000	22,000
Gross Margin	82,000	18,000	68,000
Operating Expenses			
Selling Expenses			
Marketing research	8,000	4,000	14,000
Salary	16,000	4,400	12,500
Advertising	4,200	2,050	6,400
Distribution	14,000	3,600	9,300
Maintenance	6,200	590	2,100
Miscellaneous	2,300	1,050	5,800
Total Selling Expense	$50,700	$15,690	$50,100
G and A Expenses			
Rent expense (prorated by product)	7,950	1,950	5,100
Insurance expense (prorated by product)	1,325	325	850
Depreciation (prorated by product)	3,180	780	2,040
Total G and A Expenses	$12,455	$ 3,055	$ 7,990
Total Operating Expenses	$63,155	$18,745	$58,090
Net Profit (Loss) before Taxes	$18,845	$ (745)	$ 9,910

lines are well defined in the marketing plan, the marketing manager works with sales personnel to determine when, where, and how much of the product will be sold in each region. They consider factors such as these:

- Market demand.
- Product availability.
- Competitive activity.
- Customer brand acceptance.
- Market saturation.
- Life cycle stage.
- Product monitoring.
- Other.

You will notice that these factors were researched in product positioning (Chapter 3) and portfolio analysis (Chapter 4). However, for forecasting purposes, you may need to quantify your data further.

Techniques for forecasting demand, revenue, and so on vary from relatively simple to highly sophisticated econometric models. If your current forecasting methods are inadequate, you may want to consider changing them.

Forecasts will need to be made on a product-by-product basis once you begin to develop budget figures at the tactical level. Categories at the product level are concerned solely with tactical issues. These are summed up as the budget moves up the planning ladder. The categories get broader and have more strategic applications.

Product managers must keep the positioning analysis in mind during budget development so that their budget requests reflect future product positioning strategies. For example, mature Cash Cow products would not necessarily require a high advertising budget to maintain their product position.

These predictions provide next year's forecasts of sales performance. Once the tactical budget and forecasts are made, they are summed and placed in a single pro forma statement for the final marketing plan. However, since we are concerned in this chapter with the strategic level of budget and forecasting, we will leave the tactical details out of our discussion.

One word of caution. Make sure that salespeople and product managers do not overstate their expected sales to impress top management or understate them to avoid future criticism. Inaccurate forecasting is a common cause of ineffective market planning. Stress the need for accurate, reliable estimates for budget and forecast development.

Product Contribution

When developing budget and forecast statements for individual products at the strategic level, the first item to consider is how much gross contribution the product generates and its level of contribution margin. To determine these figures, follow these steps:

- Calculate the revenues or price that each product commands within each product line.

- Determine the variable costs for each product.

- Determine the overhead/fixed cost associated with each product.

An example of calculating gross product contribution and contribution margin is shown in Figure 8.3, which depicts the historical and projected revenue and cost by each product. These calculations give you the amount of contribution dollars being generated by each of the products. You will need to determine the gross and net contributions

Figure 8.3   Historical and Projected Data (Single Product)

Variance	Row	1990	1991	1992	1993
1. Total market–units		2,800,000	3,000,000	3,400,000	3,600,000
2. Percent of total market		.12	.14	.19	.16
3. Sales in units	1 × 2	336,000	420,000	646,000	576,000
4. Price per unit		$6.00	$6.60	$7.10	$6.70
5. Variable cost per unit		$3.60	$3.90	$4.20	$3.70
6. Gross contribution margin per unit	4 – 5	$2.40	$2.70	$2.90	$3.00
7. Total dollar sales	4 × 3	$2,016,000	$2,772,000	$4,586,600	$3,859,200
8. Gross contribution margin	6 × 3	$ 806,400	$1,134,000	$1,873,400	$1,728,000
9. Overhead expenses		$ 40,000	$ 40,000	$ 40,000	$ 40,000
10. Net contribution margin	8 – 9	$ 766,400	$1,094,000	$1,833,400	$1,688,000
11. Marketing research expense		$ 110,000	$ 70,000	$ 30,000	$ 10,000
12. Salary expense		$ 310,000	$ 415,800	$ 687,900	$ 578,880
13. Advertising expense		$ 240,000	$ 332,000	$ 550,400	$ 463,100
14. Distribution expense		$ 80,000	$ 110,800	$ 183,600	$ 154,370
15. Net Operating Profit (Loss)	10 – 11 – 12 – 13 – 14	$ 26,400	$ 165,400	$ 381,500	$ 481,650

Source: Philip Kotler, *Marketing Management: Analysis, Planning, and Control,* 5th ed. (Englewood Cliffs, N.J.: Prentice-Hall, 1984): 283. Copyright 1984. Adapted by permission of Prentice-Hall.

of every product in your portfolio. The calculations can be done fairly quickly on the computer, using appropriate software.

At this point you should clearly understand why it is appropriate to start with the product line as the basis for developing your marketing plan data. You should be able to analyze your company's past performance and determine how much of each product has been sold within a given time frame. With this information, you can quickly see which products represent major sources of contribution and which do not.

Once the gross and net contributions have been calculated, the net contributions of all products can be entered on the product-line matrix. An example of a product-line matrix is shown in Figure 8.4. After you have filled out these forms, look for unusual patterns when comparing the contribution ratios with product positions on the product-line matrix.

For example, you might assume that a high-priced, high-quality product will command a higher contribution margin than a low-priced, low-quality product. Generally, as a product's quality and price increase, the incremental costs do not rise as rapidly. Thus, you would expect to see the product's contribution margin increase along with its quality and price.

Figure 8.4   Product Line Matrix—Contribution Dollars (All Products)

Product Line	Gross Contribution Margin	Net Contribution Margin
A		
1		
2		
3		
.		
.		
.		
B		
1		
2		
3		
.		
.		
.		
C		
1		
2		
3		
.		
.		
.		

However, that assumption does not always hold true since a number of variables can influence contribution margin. The benefit of viewing all products as a portfolio is that you are able to see each product's performance in relation to the others and analyze the product line(s) as a whole.

The concept of analyzing product contribution is a powerful factor in the successful implementation of any marketing plan. A product contribution margin of 30 percent to 40 percent is an appropriate range for a typical manufacturing and marketing effort.

If the business is extremely capital intensive with high fixed manufacturing costs or spends a great deal on expense categories such as advertising and promotion (as many consumer product companies do), then a much higher contribution margin should be established. On the other hand, a business that is not capital intensive would have contribution margins below the 30 percent to 40 percent range.

As a general rule, contribution margins below the 15 percent range make it difficult to generate a profit. Companies do not earn money on the basis of their contribution ratios or margins but by generating contribution dollars that, when accumulated, are greater than the total fixed costs of the business.

Establishing a Budget

In general, firms tend to use one of three methods to establish their budget: the mechanical method, task method, or group method. The main appeal of the first two methods is that they require the least amount of work.

In the *mechanical method* the budget is simply handed down as an historical cost percent or simple computation of what is left after all manufacturing costs, taxes, profits, and general and administration (G and A) items are accounted for.

In the *task method* the budget is built from the bottom up as lower levels of management estimate what they will need to perform their specific tasks. The budget is approved or rejected by upper management. However, management has little idea how the budget was actually put together; they simply give it a rubber-stamp approval or rejection.

These techniques are not in harmony with developing and using a proactive marketing plan. They simply reflect what has happened in the past. A proactive marketing plan needs a future-oriented approach that can help meet objectives and strategies developed through a close examination of the marketplace, market conditions, opportunities, voids, and portfolio interaction of products.

The *group method* is a more modern approach to establishing a budget, one that overcomes the pitfalls of the mechanical and task methods. It begins with top management sending down an overall budget estimate, based on corporate objectives, to be used as a planning guide for the allocation of marketing funds.

The marketing manager develops strategies that remain within the general limits of that estimate. However, the manager is also free to recommend exceptions that go beyond those limits, backed up by full details justifying all requests. In the end, top management reviews the marketing plan and its detailed marketing budget(s) and reaches a final approved figure.

This method is more time consuming than the other two and requires considerable communication between various department heads and top management. However, the benefits outweigh the cost. The group method of establishing a budget enables the marketing plan to be communicated to many areas, both inside and outside the marketing department. In addition, top management gains a clear idea of the costs required to reach the proposed marketing strategies and objectives described in the final plan.

Allocating the Marketing Budget

Assigning specific budget figures to strategies and marketing activities can be a difficult task. Firms may use certain mathematical models for this step, depending on their level of sophistication.

As a general rule of thumb, start with the strategies and marketing activities that have the most reliable set of historical or projected data available, for example, historical personnel costs, cost per sales call, advertising expenses, and purchasing. This historical information gives you a base for predicting the future. However, be sure that budget allocations support your product portfolio strategies designed to achieve your three-year objectives.

As you work through the budget process, you will come across new items or items with insufficient historical data to use as a basis for estimating budget requirements. In these cases, you will have to rely on the judgment of a good seasoned market planner.

The following questions should help you develop a well-balanced and workable budget. If you find yourself unable to answer most of those marked with an asterisk (∗), you may need to reexamine your original basic data analysis and strategy development. There may be too many gaps in the data, or the early procedures may not have been adequately performed.

This fact underscores the importance of taking your time to develop carefully your basic data and the strategies drawn from positioning analyses. You will be required to support the budget request to carry out those strategies successfully.

Among the questions you need to answer are these:

- Is the amount of money requested sufficient to achieve a stated objective through the strategies that have been developed?

- If more money is required to meet objectives, from which activities can it be appropriated?

- Is the profit contribution potential of a given product in line with the budget request?

∗ Does the potential for profit justify requesting additional funds from top management?

∗ Are there any alternative strategies that can achieve an equally favorable end result at a lower cost?

∗ Are the costs allocated realistically, given the product's life cycle analysis?

∗ Does the budget adequately cover all the necessary elements of the marketing mix?

If the budget is not carefully prepared—i.e., is incomplete, has poor forecasts, contains conflicting requests—it is quite possible that top management will reduce the size of the budget. Or they may ask for a major revision, which is costly because it ties up departmental and top management's time to review the revised budget.

Lack of budget planning can seriously affect the firm's ability to achieve the strategic objectives and strategies in the marketing plan and may cause the entire plan to fail. On the other hand, a well-prepared and supported budgetary plan can help to obtain the necessary allocations of money and resources from top management to implement the marketing plan to the fullest.

When upper management review the forecast and budget, they may ask for modifications. Keep in mind that for any modifications requiring a reduction in expenses, you must reevaluate the strategies that may be affected. You will need to reformulate those strategies to fit the new constraints in the budget.

Once top management approve the strategic budget, it becomes part of the marketing plan. It serves as the basis for material procurement, production scheduling, personnel planning, and marketing operations.

Pitfalls to Avoid

Two major pitfalls to avoid in developing your budget and forecasting deserve mention. One has to do with inflating the budget and the other with milking it dry.

In many companies today, there is an unfortunate trend to inflate the budget artificially as estimates are being developed. This happens for a simple reason: many planners know that when their budget is sent up for approval it will be cut by a certain percent. If an inflated budget is cut, the planner still ends up with the correct amount to implement the marketing plan successfully. The inflation game is likely to continue for some time to come, mainly because of planners who cannot estimate expenses correctly and cannot control their budget.

One way to avoid playing this nonproductive game is to build a contingency fund into the budget to provide for unexpected expenses. The contingency fund would be used only when necessary. Including these funds in the budget provides a more accurate picture of the true budget needed to implement the plan.

The other pitfall arises when planners discover they are running under budget. The temptation is to spend all the funds in the budget for fear that the next year's allocations will automatically be lowered. However, keep in mind that the goal of each department is to save the firm expense dollars and add to the company's total profitability.

You can avoid this pitfall by explaining why you were running under budget. Perhaps the reduction in expenses was due to a one-time windfall, such as an unexpected surge in demand or the loss of a major competitor. This could result in a significant drop in advertising expenses and an increase in sales growth.

Make sure your projected budget requests are tied to future objectives and strategies, not entirely to historical data projections, and you are much more likely to have your requests approved. The past may not be congruent with the new strategic path you are setting, particularly if you are changing the company's direction.

The group method of establishing budgets can help prevent companies from either artificially inflating or using up their budgets. By eliminating these two pitfalls, you can improve the financial health and marketing success of the firm. The budget and forecasting process must show the firm where it is going, not simply where it has been.

Summary

- While strategies outline a firm's plan of attack, the budget specifies how much it will cost. It is important to remember, however, that drawing up a budget is not the same as strategic planning. Budgets simply provide control, monitor expenses, track revenue, and so on.

- The first step in developing a budget at the strategic level is to identify your own department's area of fiscal responsibility, looking at two broad categories of total marketing costs: (1) order-getting and (2) order-filling costs. The marketing plan is almost entirely concerned with the order-getting process.

- The second step is to obtain budget estimates from each department in the firm associated with marketing activities, organizing the budget into discrete categories, preferably by marketing function responsibility.

- The marketing department is responsible for preparing a budget statement that reflects projected costs associated with the developed marketing plan as well as a revenue/sales forecast.

- A simplified corporate budget statement is essentially a projected profit and loss statement. An individual product budget statement is developed at the marketing department level.

- Once the product lines are well defined in the marketing plan, the marketing manager works with sales personnel and company forecasters to predict product demand and sales performance.

- Forecasts are made on a product-by-product basis once you begin to develop budget figures at the tactical level. These are summed up as the budget moves up the corporate ladder.

- When developing budget and forecast statements for individual products at the strategic level, the first item to consider is how large a gross contribution the product generates and its level of contribution margin. The concept of analyzing product contribution is a powerful factor in the successful implementation of any marketing plan.

- Firms tend to establish their budget using one of three methods: mechanical method, task method, or group method. Although the group method requires more time, it enables the marketing plan to be communicated to many areas and gives top management a clear idea of the costs required to reach proposed marketing strategies and objectives.

- In assigning specific budget figures to strategies and marketing activities, start with those that have the most reliable set of historical or projected data available.

- Two pitfalls to avoid in developing the budget and forecasting are artificially inflating budget estimates and spending all unused funds before the end of the fiscal year. These two trends distort budget estimates.

Sample Case
Budgeting for Growth

Haines had learned from his research on DataStar that the budget was generally put together through the task method. Managers estimated their budget needs, and the finance department put the figures together. Upper management approved the budget but had little idea how it was created. The budget was not future oriented but simply reflected what had been done in the past.

Haines called a meeting with top management to discuss the group method of developing the budget for the new marketing plan. He had to convince the three partners to become more involved in the process and, to help create a budget estimate based on corporate objectives.

This estimate would be used as a planning guide for allocating marketing funds. All department heads and product managers, in turn, would develop their own budget estimates, using the top management estimate as a guide. Haines and his marketing team would work with the finance staff to coordinate all these estimates and to create the final budget figures for the marketing plan.

Simic agreed at once, much to Haines's surprise. "Financial categories are something solid; I can work with them better than I can with objectives and strategies," Simic said.

But Price and Koster were less enthusiastic about the idea. They did not want to get involved in the details of developing budget estimates. Haines suggested they work with Simic and the finance department to make the job easier, and they reluctantly agreed.

A draft copy of corporate marketing objectives and strategies would be distributed to all department heads and managers to help them devise their budgets. Top management would have the Business Plan as well.

"I'm also revising the budget format since the current one doesn't show enough detail. The new format, with a finer breakdown of categories, will help in decision making and control procedures. We'll be able to track and analyze our financial statements more easily."

Haines then outlined what the product managers would need to do to create their own budget estimates for each product.

"They'll have to provide a contribution analysis of each product and develop their own profit and loss statement. The marketing department will review these statements and then sum each individual budget into an overall marketing budget that will be included in the final marketing plan.

"Forecasts of revenue by product will be done by the forecasting group in finance. The product managers will review these forecasts to make sure that all pertinent variables have been included and that the forecasts are reasonable. Just as the sum of all budgets by department equals the corporate budget, the total of all sales forecasts by product will equal the corporate revenue forecast.

"In the final step, top management will review and approve all budget items. I realize this process will take more time than the old way, but it involves everyone in creating estimates and budgets. People are much more willing to accept final budget allocations when they've had a hand in developing them."

Over the next two weeks, Haines and his team coordinated their efforts with the finance department to assist department heads and product managers in their budget estimates. Haines wanted to make sure that no budget was inflated and that budget categories truly reflected the new strategies and objectives, not simply last year's allocations.

The completed Projected Profit and Loss Statement and the Forecasted Sales and Profit Data for AutoDrive (as shown in abbreviated form following) provide examples of the individual product estimates Haines used in creating a marketing budget. He and his marketing team received similar data for all products. The final budget was included in the marketing plan.

		Product:		AutoDrive	

Projected Profit and Loss Statement as of 12/31/91

Revenues			$7,905,000
Cost of goods sold			4,473,000
Gross Margin			$3,432,000
Operating Expenses			
Selling Expenses			
Advertising expense	$633,000		
Distribution expense	474,000		
Market research expense	125,000		
Sales salary expense	210,000		
Miscellaneous expenses	30,000		
Total Selling Expenses		$1,472,000	
General and Administrative Expenses			
Office salaries expense	$ 74,250		
Rent expense	14,500		
Insurance expense	1,800		
Supplies	5,600		
Depreciation expense	13,850		
Total G and A Expenses		$ 110,000	
Total Operating Expenses			$1,582,000
Net Profit (Loss) before Taxes			$1,850,000

Note: All expenses have been identified directly to the product or allocated accordingly.

3–Year Forecasted Sales and Profit Data

	Row	1994	1995	1996
1. Market—total units		85,000	93,500	102,847
2. Market share percent		.12	.24	.36
3. Price per unit $		775	725	630
4. Variable cost per unit $		465	435	380
5. Gross contribution margin per unit $	3–4	310	290	250
6. Sales volume in units	1 × 2	10,200	22,440	37,025
7. Sales $	3 × 6	7,905,000	16,269,000	23,325,750
8. Gross contribution margin $	5 × 6	3,162,000	6,507,600	9,256,250
9. Overhead $ to this product		110,000	110,000	120,000
10. Net contribution margin $	8 – 9	3,052,000	6,397,600	9,136,250
11. Advertising $		633,000	1,302,000	2,180,000
12. Distribution $		474,000	1,092,000	1,675,000
13. Marketing research $		125,000	80,000	30,000
14. Sales salaries $		210,000	240,000	180,000
15. Miscellaneous expenses $		30,000	30,000	30,000
16. Net Operating Profit (Loss)	10 – 11 – 12 – 13 – 14 – 15	$1,580,000	$3,653,600	$ 5,041,250

PART FOUR

Implementation and Control

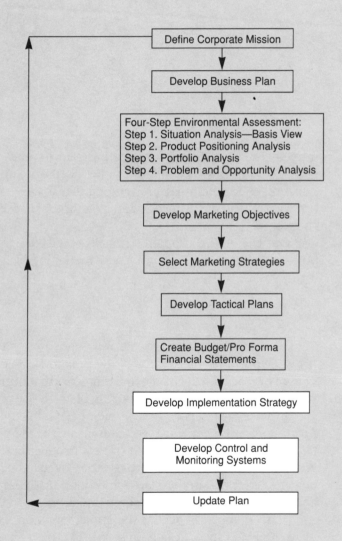

CHAPTER NINE

Implementation

Introduction

Implementing the finished marketing plan requires a strategy all its own. To be successful, implementation needs the support of top management, good communication among all managers and staff, close coordination of all departments, and a method of handling resistance to change.

Our goal in this chapter is to help you to design an implementation strategy that will give your new marketing plan the best chance for success.

Implementation

Implementation is that part of market planning that is also a component of organizational change. It is a process that begins with the company's first ideas for a new marketing plan.

In a very real sense, then, implementation is the *art of introducing and managing change.* For example, does the plan call for entering a new market or developing a new product line? Is a new R & D group to be formed? Does the sales group need to be reorganized? Any changes described in the plan will require that company procedures and personnel adjust to fit the new direction.

Many companies believe the implementation stage will take care of itself. This can be a fatal mistake. The best marketing plans can flounder on any one of a number of problems.

Problem Areas in Implementation

There are several reasons why marketing plans are not successfully implemented when completed.

- Faulty design of the plan. For example, some marketing plans do not provide the information needed by company management and staff to implement the plans successfully. Different plans and strategies are needed for different tasks.

- Poor communication with department heads and personnel. If users of a marketing plan see it only after it's finished, they may feel the plan is unrealistic for their departments. Managers and their staffs should be consulted in the initial planning stages. Poor communication not only can result in planning errors but can create determined resistance to the plan itself.

- Lack of interest in the plan at top management levels. Top management must take the lead in implementing and supporting the new plan. If they show a lack of interest or indicate that the plan is not important, line managers and support personnel will not take it seriously either.

- Lack of resources to carry out the plan. The resources required to fulfill the plan must not be beyond the scope of the firm. Managers and support personnel cannot be asked to do too much too quickly. Faulty or myopic planning can sink a new marketing plan in the early stages of implementation.

Most of these problems can be traced to poor communication between planners and top management, department heads, and support staff. It is crucial to involve all levels of company personnel in the planning process from the very first stages. This process stresses the importance of planning from the bottom up as well as from the top down.

Implementation Strategy

Your new marketing plan represents two types of change: (1) organizational—new procedures, products, work routines, areas of business, and (2) behavioral—changes in employee attitudes, skills, routines.

You will need to establish a clear-cut strategy to introduce and manage these changes. Although the situation will differ for each company, the following strategy outline should hold true across the board.

1. Gain top management approval and support for the final plan.

2. Have top management present the plan as the company blueprint for successful change to managers and support staff.

3. Assign specific implementation tasks to department heads and managers.

4. Set schedules and target dates for completion of implementation tasks (new procedures in place, new department formed, new sales approach in use).

5. Establish regular training and feedback sessions to train employees in new routines and procedures, resolve conflicts, and obtain feedback on implementation.

Each step is discussed more fully below.

Top Management Support

We cannot stress too strongly the importance of gaining top management approval of and commitment to the new marketing plan. It is perhaps the key element in implementation strategy. Top management can perform five essential tasks in the implementation process:

1. Communicate the plan to their peers and to the entire company.

2. Describe why the changes contained in the plan are necessary, what impact these changes will have on individual departments, and what results can be expected from implementing the new plan.

3. Allocate the necessary resources (money, staff, materials) to carry out all implementation steps.

4. Be present at all major decision-making sessions.

5. Resolve conflicts among peers and mediate any power struggles. Without top management leadership, interdepartmental disputes can paralyze an implementation process. With their commitment, it is much easier to resolve differences, deal with problem areas, and keep the strategic goals of the plan firmly in mind.

Ideally, these tasks have been ongoing throughout the design stage of the plan and can continue into the implementation phase.

Presenting the Marketing Plan to the Company

Top management should schedule a general meeting or series of meetings with department heads to present the plan and explain how it will affect individual departments. Invite discussion and questions at these meetings. Make sure that everyone has a common understanding of the plan.

The method of communicating the plan will vary according to the size and organizational structure of each company. In some firms, top management may send a general memorandum to all department personnel summarizing the new marketing plan and explaining its impact on each department. In others, department heads will be responsible for explaining to their staffs how the new plan will affect their areas.

Assigning Implementation Tasks

Avoid distributing a master copy of the plan to all managers. High-level strategic plans should be kept at top management level for security reasons. For example, if the entire plan is widely distributed, anyone leaving the company, from executives to sales reps, could carry the plan with them.

Each person involved in implementation should receive only the part needed to perform his or her duties effectively. Everyone should know clearly what is expected of them and why. Each manager in turn can share appropriate parts of the plan with subordinates on a need-to-know basis. This approach also helps top management better coordinate and control the entire implementation process.

One of the most effective ways to implement a new plan is by forming committees. Committees may be set up within a department or among two or more departments to help coordinate implementation steps. Reorganizing the sales force, for example, could involve the sales, marketing, and finance departments. A joint committee could help smooth the transition from the old procedures to the new ones.

Setting Schedules and Target Dates

Every implementation task should have a schedule and target date for completion. These schedules and target dates should be coordinated by top management. If the sales force is to be reorganized within six months, then the new marketing materials must be ready and the new compensation system in place at the same time.

Implementation committees can help to ensure open communication among departments and to resolve problems as they arise. Top management should be available to settle disputes that cannot be handled in committees or among staff themselves.

Establishing Training and Feedback Sessions

If the change involves introducing new procedures, office equipment, and high-tech systems, make sure that staff are given adequate training. Change is disturbing in itself, but particularly so when people must learn new skills. By giving employees the knowledge and practice time they need to become proficient, you can greatly ease the transition from one system to another and minimize the loss of productive time.

Also, schedule feedback sessions to keep all participants advised of progress in implementing the new plan and the accomplishments that have been achieved. Change is often easier to tolerate if people understand they are making progress toward a specific goal. These sessions can give employees an opportunity to offer suggestions or to point out problems in the early stages of the implementation process.

Managing the Behavioral Side of Change

Your implementation strategy should also take into account some of the behavioral aspects of change. How do you gain people's cooperation and compliance? What motivates people to accept change? How can you avoid some of the miscommunication that seems inevitable whenever change is introduced?

People resist change for many reasons. They fear losing what they have; they dislike disruption in routine; they fear being asked to learn new and seemingly complex skills; they fear losing their jobs, getting a pay cut, or being demoted. Those who introduce change can help to ease the transition by telling people what the change involves and how it will affect them.

While an in-depth study of human behavior and change is beyond the scope of this book, we can offer you a few guidelines in three key areas: preventing resistance to change, identifying motivations, and meeting people's different communication needs. These guidelines can help you avoid or deal with some of the behavioral problems that often arise when companies introduce change into their organization.

User Participation

Organizational psychologists have suggested that one of the most successful ways to approach change is through *user participation,* that is, involving people in the process from its early stages. A number of experiments and field studies have been conducted using this technique. In each case, the results supported the importance of user participation in any implementation strategy. Some reasons include:

• Participation enhances the self-esteem of those included in the process. They feel important and tend to express more positive attitudes toward change.

• Participation can be challenging and intrinsically satisfying to workers whose jobs are routine or fairly predictable. These workers are also likely to express positive attitudes toward change.

- Participating users learn more about the upcoming change as the planning process moves from stage to stage. They become familiar with the plan's details and are usually better trained to implement it.

- Participation improves the overall quality of results achieved through the change. Participants understand more clearly how and why the new plan is an improvement over the old one.

- Participants usually retain more control over their activities during the change. Research has shown that this sense of control is an important factor in developing positive attitudes toward change.

If managers and workers are part of the planning process from the beginning and are consulted throughout the planning stages, they tend to have greater ownership of the new plan and are more interested in seeing it implemented successfully.

Motivation

You are also more likely to persuade people to accept change if you know something about what motivates them. People will want to know how the new plan will benefit them. Some basic concerns motivating people in a business environment include the following:

Profit — improving it

Saving — spending less

Prestige — position and pride

Self-esteem — preserving a sense of self-worth

Security — knowing what to expect

Comfort — feeling of well being

Convenience — saving time, boosting efficiency

Health — maintaining or improving it

Productivity — increasing it

Loyalty — fidelity to others, oneself

Curiosity — a sense of wonder, risk taking

While people may be motivated by a combination of concerns in the above list, usually one will be dominant. Once you know the strongest motivator for the key people involved in implementation, you can pinpoint the benefits they will derive from the change. For example, a manager motivated primarily by productivity will want to know how the plan is going to save employee time, enable staff to work more efficiently, and streamline work steps.

People who feel the new plan is satisfying a primary motivator are usually more willing to endure the temporary upheaval that accompanies any change in company procedures, direction, or mission.

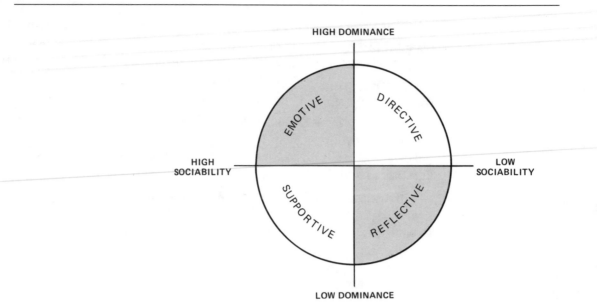

Figure 9.1 Mok's Communication Style Model

Communication Style Model

Many people resist change largely because of miscommunication rather than because of the disruption in routine the change represents. Just as everyone is motivated by different concerns, so everyone has a different communication style.

You can improve your chances of gaining people's cooperation if you communicate change to them in a way they can understand, a way that satisfies their communication needs. For example, some people feel overwhelmed if told all the details of a new procedure at the beginning; others need to know all the steps in advance before they attempt to learn the first one. By learning something about the various communication needs of key personnel in the company, you can tailor your presentation to meet those needs.

Psychologist Paul Mok, an expert in how people communicate in organizations, has developed a Communication Style Model that identifies four basic communication styles: emotive, directive, supportive, and reflective. According to Mok, people have various combinations of high and low *sociability* (how they interact with people) and high and low *dominance* (their need for control in a situation). By charting these variables, he has identified the basic characteristics of the four styles, as shown in Figure 9.1.

Emotive Style. People with an *emotive style* of communication possess high sociability and high dominance. They are emotional, vivid personalities who command attention and respect in any group. They are oriented toward action, like informality, and possess a natural persuasiveness. They do not necessarily need to know the details of a plan, only the actions to be taken and the end results expected. They are likely to read the summary of the plan and leave the details to others.

Directive Style. Those with a *directive style* of communication have high dominance combined with low sociability. They are generally frank, demanding, aggressive, and determined. Sentiment plays little part in their thinking. They generally project a serious attitude, express strong opinions, and may seem aloof or distant to their staff. They will want to know what data you have to support the strategies in the new plan and the rationale for any changes or new directions that have been recommended.

Reflective Style. People with a *reflective style* are characterized by low sociability and low dominance. Reflective communicators are usually quiet, enjoy working on their own, and make decisions only after considerable deliberation. They tend to want detailed explanations of any new procedures and enjoy scrutinizing the fine print. They prefer orderliness, often seem preoccupied, and express their opinions in a formal, deliberate manner. In many instances, people with a reflective communication style are in the more technical fields where attention to detail is a strong suit.

Supportive Style. Those with a *supportive style* rate low in dominance and high in sociability. They are people oriented, sensitive, and patient; and they are generally good listeners. They tend to avoid the overt use of power and rely on friendly persuasion in dealing with people. Their decisions are made and expressed in a thoughtful, deliberate manner. Supportive style communicators tend to be concerned with the impact of a new plan on their staff or on the company's employees, in addition to the more technical aspects of the proposed changes.

By identifying people's basic communication styles, you can present the new marketing plan in ways that satisfy their communication needs. If the marketing plan calls for developing a new product line, the directive communicator will want to know what facts and figures justify the risk. On the other hand, an emotive communicator may want to know potential rewards for such a risk. The reflective communicator will want details about research and development, time lines, raw materials, and production schedules. The supportive communicator may be concerned about extra demands on the workers.

It can be well worth your time to learn something about the primary motivations and basic communication styles of the people who must implement the new marketing plan. Introducing and managing change is not easy under the best of circumstances. Some background work on your part can help give the new marketing plan the best chance for success.

Measuring Success

How do you know when you have successfully implemented a plan? Researchers have not really agreed on any one indicator for successful implementation. However, we suggest two methods for judging whether the process is accomplishing your implementation goals.

A cost-benefit study can be used to measure tangible costs and benefits. In this evaluation, you total the cost of developing the plan and compare it with the dollar benefits resulting from implementing it. Data for a cost-benefit analysis can be obtained from monthly sales and cost reports, cash flows, and monthly pro forma statements.

But a cost-benefit approach is not very useful in evaluating the *intangible* costs and benefits of a new marketing plan. Your plan may be highly proactive and contain procedures the firm has never used before. You may be looking three to five years into the future with no immediate, measurable results for several months. For example, a plan for improving customer relations may initially cost the company more than it receives in increased orders. But in the long run the plan will achieve the goals of improving customer relations and, hopefully, increasing sales.

In such cases, you may be able to evaluate your implementation strategy by determining *users' level of satisfaction* in implementing the plan. High levels of satisfaction generally indicate high levels of use regarding new procedures, systems, and policies. Ask managers and support staff for specific comments on the implementation process. Is the plan meeting the strategies and objectives of each department? Are people accepting the changes or trying to go back to their old ways? Has it made decision making easier? Are employees positive about the new direction the company is taking?

Answers to these questions will give you an idea of how the initial implementation process is going. This approach can help detect problems early, whether in procedures or behavior, before they become serious enough to threaten the success of the entire program.

Form 9: Implementation Strategy will help you to identify key steps you need to take in implementing your new marketing plan. This rough outline can also help you to anticipate potential organizational and behavioral problems that may arise during implementation and to develop suggested strategies for avoiding or dealing with them.

In the next chapter, we discuss how to set up control and monitoring procedures for longer term evaluation of the new marketing plan.

Summary

- Implementation is that part of market planning that is also a component of organizational change. To be successful, implementation requires the support of top management, good communication among managers and staff, close coordination of all departments, and some methods for handling resistance to change.

- Problem areas in implementation include faulty design of the plan, poor communication with department heads and personnel, lack of top management interest in the plan, and lack of resources to carry out the plan.

- In general, the strategy for implementing the marketing plan includes (1) gaining top management approval and support, (2) having top management present the plan to managers and staff, (3) assigning specific implementation tasks, (4) setting schedules and target dates for implementation tasks, and (5) establishing training and feedback sessions.

- To manage many of the problems that arise when introducing change into an organization, it is wise to involve managers and staff early in the planning process, know something about what motivates them, and gain some understanding of their individual communication styles.

- Mok's Communication Style Model identifies four distinct styles: emotive, directive, reflective, and supportive. Each style has different needs for sociability and dominance.

- Two methods can help you to judge the progress of your implementation strategy: a cost-benefit study and determining users' level of satisfaction with the changes introduced.

Sample Case   Setting the Plan in Motion

The final marketing plan was printed and bound, and the marketing team breathed a sigh of relief. Haines, however, reminded them that only half the job had been done. Now they needed to develop an implementation strategy for the plan to make sure it had the best chance of succeeding. Haines had learned from experience that this step was one of the most critical and most frequently overlooked in the entire planning process.

"You need to understand," Haines told his worried team, "that designing a marketing plan means asking people to change organizational procedures and their own behavior."

"How are we going to plan implementation steps for so many different departments?" one member asked.

Haines laughed. "Relax. We've already done a lot of work on this step. Now you're going to see the benefits of all your efforts to involve people in the planning process these past few months."

Haines outlined how their previous work would help to ensure that the marketing plan would be implemented successfully.

- The design of the plan revolved around the Mission Statement and Business Plan, which made it compatible from the outset with the direction and purpose of the company.

- Top management had been involved from the beginning and had supported Haines and the marketing team every step of the way.

- All department heads, product managers, and staffs had been included in planning meetings and had reviewed and revised draft plans before the final plan was developed.

- Haines had obtained the necessary resources early on to carry out the plan.

"As a result," Haines said, "the impact of organizational and behavioral changes should be minimal. Top management will support the plan and present it as the blueprint of the company. However, there's always some resistance to change, so we need to consider who's likely to give us trouble and how to handle their objections or resistance. Any ideas?"

"Yes," one team member replied. "We're going to be introducing telemarketing to the sales department. The clerical staff will be doing the phone work and passing on leads to the field sales force. In my experience, unless the change is handled carefully, there's usually friction between the clerical staff and field sales force. Paul Sandler, the assistant sales manager, will be in charge of the training sessions; and he's pretty much of a by-the-book guy. I'm not sure he's going to see the potential conflicts in the changes."

"All right, let's do a little strategizing on this. How would you characterize Paul's communication style?"

"Definitely directive with some reflective thrown in. He's very thorough when he develops a program and often teaches it himself. I've heard that he's a hard taskmaster."

"How can we present the potential conflicts we see in his department so that he'll hear them?" Haines asked.

"Well . . . I think the best approach is to put it in terms of efficiency. If a training program can be designed that will prevent clashes between the clerical staff and field sales force, the telemarketing system will be implemented faster, with a shorter learning curve, and fewer problems on the job."

"What about the clerical staff and sales force—what are the basic conflicts that come up between them?" Haines asked.

"The clerical staff usually haven't done any selling, so they don't understand how much time it takes to sell different clients. They often load too many calls on the sales force. The sales force, on the other hand, feel they've lost some of their autonomy and prestige by taking orders from clerks. They tend to see their new responsibilities as a step down."

"So how can we handle these problems?" Haines wanted to know.

The team members started throwing out suggestions.

"We can tell them that when the clerical staff screens leads, their chances of closing a sale go up. They don't have to make nearly as many cold calls or go after questionable prospects."

"Yes, the more closings, the more commissions they'll earn. They can boost their income."

"We can introduce a new incentive system, maybe one based on clerical/sales force teamwork as well as individual sales efforts."

"Good ideas," Haines said. "Once the plan is approved, we can set up a meeting with the sales manager and Sandler. Any other problem areas?"

"I know a big one," another team member said. "Ms. Koster and Mr. Simic aren't going to like the fact that engineering won't be driving the company as much. Even though they've backed us all the way, when it gets down to implementing the changes this plan advocates, I think they're going to resist following some of the marketing objectives. They've always had control over the product lines, and we're taking over some of that function."

"Good point," Haines said. "This is a delicate issue. We want to prevent conflicts between ourselves and top management and at the same time stand by the marketing objectives and strategies that have been developed. That means we may have to be in the hot seat at times."

"Do you think there will be any in-fighting among the three partners?"

Haines replied, "Part of our job will be to help prevent a breakdown in communication among the partners."

"How do we do that?" one of the team members asked.

"By keeping them all involved in the implementation process as much as possible. They'll have a chance to air any objections or problems before the issues get too big to handle. Remember, we have one fact working in our favor. Their old way of operating got the company in trouble to begin with. If they try to go back to that way, the same problems will crop up. The changes in the marketing plan will correct those problems and help the company grow. It'll be hard for them to dispute that fact, but we need to present this point of view in a way that respects their concerns and interests."

"I know one thing; Ms. Koster has a reflective communication style while Mr. Simic is more directive. She'll want to know the details of why we need to follow the marketing objectives, while he'll just want to know the end results."

"We can prepare for both each time we meet with them," Haines said. "Any more problem areas we need to cover?"

The team suggested a few more in the production and finance department, and Haines helped them to develop strategies to handle these potential problems.

"All right, we have to develop a list of top management personnel who need to approve the plan, a timetable for presentations, and a list of potential problems along with the strategies we've brainstormed for each one. At this point it's important to keep the problems and strategies confidential. We don't want people feeling that we're singling them out as potential troublemakers.

"Once the marketing plan is officially launched, we'll help each department set implementation goals to coordinate the process on a company-wide basis. The marketing department is the official liaison and communications link among all departments and management levels."

Haines and his team completed Form 9 Implementation Strategy and submitted only the implementation schedule to the three partners for approval. While only two problem areas are presented on the form for the purposes of illustration, the list would actually include all potential problems and the strategies developed to handle them.

Form 9   Implementation Strategy

Product: <u>AutoDrive</u>   Date: _____

1. Members of top management who must approve and endorse the new marketing plan:

President—Mr. Price
_____

VP Marketing—Mr. Haines
_____

VP Operations/R & D—Mr. Simic
_____

VP Finance—Mr. Stawinski
_____

VP Engineering—Ms. Koster
_____

Manager Sales—Ms. Pittman
_____

2. Schedule of presentations:

Group	Date of Presentation
Top management	March 2
Product managers	March 3–5
Sales department	March 6
Support staff	March 9

3. Potential organizational and behavioral problems that may arise during implementation*:

(1) Change from engineering-driven to marketing-driven approach may be difficult for Ms. Koster and Mr. Simic to accept fully. They may perceive the change as a loss of control over products on their part. Mr. Simic may distrust the soundness of some marketing objectives and strategies.

(2) Introduction of telemarketing in the sales department may create conflicts between clerical and sales force staff. Mr. Sandler may not have foreseen these conflicts when developing the training program.

4. Suggested strategies for preventing or handling organizational and behavioral problems:

(1) Keep all three partners involved throughout the implementation process; facilitate communication among the partners and provide opportunities to work out problems in the early stages. Demonstrate the soundness of marketing objectives and strategies, tailoring the presentations to reflect the communication style of each partner.

(2) Meet with the sales manager and assistant manager to explain the benefits of anticipating and addressing potential conflicts between clerical and sales force staff. Meet with clerical and sales force staff to explain the changes involved in switching to telemarketing; outline the potential problem areas and benefits of this approach.

*This part of the form is kept confidential and would not be circulated with the schedule.

CHAPTER TEN

Control and Monitoring

Introduction

Once the marketing plan is implemented, controls must be developed to monitor progress and to keep the company on track toward its desired objectives. These activities are essential in order for the company to correct problems in their early stages and to measure outcomes.

Unfortunately, many companies tend to limit their control and monitoring efforts to tracking financial reports. While financial statements and return on investment relationships are important to the health of the firm, their focus is somewhat limited. This information will tell you whether your company is making money, but not necessarily whether it is making progress toward other strategic goals. You need to look at the broader picture, which includes such factors as market share, competitive analysis, and product positioning.

In short, you should have control yardsticks for every strategic objective in your plan, a standard or criterion for evaluating progress toward that objective, and tracking devices to monitor progress and help you to determine the causes of any deviations from your goals. Contingency strategies and tactics can be used to correct the company's course.

In this chapter, we discuss the key control and monitoring activities that should be performed during implementation of the marketing plan and over the long term.

Control—Concept and Purpose

Control can be defined as the actions taken to keep the firm directed toward its objectives and to bring performance and desired results closer together. Control activities involve two types of actions:

1. Monitoring departmental and individual actions to determine progress toward goals and outcomes.
2. Taking steps to ensure that performance matches desired results or to adjust your objectives to match attainable performance levels.

Control can be conducted at the *strategic level* (reshaping the programs to be implemented in the future) or at the *tactical level* (taking specific actions to keep the current plan on course). We include both levels in our discussion.

The Marketing Controller Concept

The managerial responsibility of control and monitoring is generally assigned to the person responsible for developing the marketing plan. This person oversees the entire implementation and control process, maintaining communication among departments and coordinating data to determine how deviation from plan in one area may affect other areas.

Some companies, however, are also establishing job positions known as *marketing controllers* to monitor marketing expenses and activities. Marketing controllers perform a function similar to the accounting department controller. In the accounting office, controllers conduct audits, fill out tax forms, monitor expenses and budgets, make sure all financial records are correct and performed on a timely basis, and so on.

Marketing controllers, however, are trained in both finance and marketing areas. They are usually on the same level as the marketing manager, and their duties include the following*:

- Advise management on the best timing for marketing strategies.
- Keep a record of adherence to profit plan.
- Oversee brand manager's budgets.
- Analyze media production costs.
- Measure the impact of various sales promotions.
- Evaluate customer and geographic profitability.
- Evaluate sales-oriented financial reports.
- Educate the marketing department on the financial implications of marketing decisions.

---

*Based on Sam R. Goodman, *Increasing Corporate Profitability* (New York: Ronald Press, 1982): Chapter 1.

The marketing controller concept is an intriguing one, particularly in organizations where marketing is still practiced with a primary eye toward sales rather than profits. The marketing controller can make a contribution by analyzing how and where the company is making its money as the marketing plan is carried out. This also includes monitoring actual strategies, making sure they are being implemented as written. The marketing controller informs management about any deviations from plan.

Elements in a Control System

An effective control system enables the marketing controller or planner to do the following:

- Detect when and where deviations from the planned results are occurring.
- Determine the cause of any deviations from the plan.
- Suggest ways to correct the situation, if possible, and bring activities back in line with the plan. To do so may require creating an interdepartmental task force to handle complex situations.

In order to achieve those aims, the controller or planner needs yardsticks and comparative standards, a feedback or performance information system, diagnostic ability and an analytic system, and contingency plans and methods.

Yardsticks and Comparative Standards. Yardsticks are individual goals taken from the marketing plan that serve as the basis for product and personnel performance evaluation. Yardsticks are set at the tactical level to indicate what should happen when the plan is being met.

For example, a company may set a goal to increase market share by 8 percent by the end of the third quarter. If by the end of the second quarter market share is up only 2 percent, the original figure serves as a yardstick for the manager, indicating the company may be off course.

The final marketing plan should contain clearly stated yardsticks so that deviations or problems can be detected early and timely actions taken through the use of contingency plans.

Feedback or Performance Information System. The feedback or performance information system should provide frequent reports on results. The information system is based on various financial and other reporting forms, market research data, and personnel feedback.

Diagnostic Ability and an Analytic System. The controller or planner and individual managers must be able to diagnose problems and develop a system to analyze the situation and to determine the underlying cause or causes. This depends not only on their personal insights, experience, and problem-solving abilities but also on the availability of information regarding external and internal marketing activities.

While individual managers will diagnose problems in their own functional areas, the controller keeps the lines of communication open among various departments. He or she consults with managers to determine the impact of a problem in one area on company activities in other areas. An increase in the price of raw materials, for example, will have a direct impact on production costs and product pricing strategies. Individual managers are responsible for notifying the controller or planner immediately when they detect problems so that corrective action can be taken.

Contingency Plans and Methods. When the company cannot achieve its desired end results, it must be able to fall back on contingency objectives and strategies. The market planner and individual managers must be able to make tactical changes to correct the diagnosed problems and to get the company back on track.

Control Guidelines

Many questions must be addressed for control purposes during the planning and implementation periods. If certain parts of implementing the actual plan begin to deviate from the formal plan, corrective action must be taken immediately. These questions include the following:

- Is market share increasing or decreasing as expected? If not, how does this affect the projected portfolio positioning?
- Are sales on track? If not, what are the dollar and percentage variances between planned and actual?
- Is the marketplace changing? If so, where and how?
- Is the return on assets and net worth meeting the firm's objectives?
- From a profitability perspective, which products should be added, deleted, or repositioned to keep the plan on track?
- Are expenses *ahead* of estimates? If so, why?
  –Have assumptions changed?
  –Should objectives be modified?
  –Have the correct strategies been selected?
  –Is competition increasing, thus lowering profits?

–Should budget cuts be considered?

–Are unforeseen outside influences causing the variances?

–Are there more effective ways to manage the sales force, advertising, distribution?

- Are expenses *behind* estimates? If so, why?

    –Are the strategies being properly carried out as planned?

    –Are the variances indicating new or expanding opportunities which were not considered or seen previously?

    –If the strategy is more effective than anticipated, should funds be added to accelerate profits further?

For example, when budget variances occur, either up or down, it is wise to reexamine your original assumptions. You may be able to pinpoint the cause for any variance and to use contingency plans and strategies to correct the situation. The budget should be flexible enough to adjust readily to changes in operating or marketing conditions (profit, cash flow, economy shifts, sales variances, expanded opportunities, seasonal factors, and competition). A thorough review of the budget should be scheduled at least monthly.

A Monitoring System

Once the basic elements of a control system are established, the company can begin monitoring the execution of the strategic marketing plan.

A monitoring system has two main parts. The first is a control and performance information system designed to provide management with data about the internal and external factors affecting implementation and the outcomes of the marketing plan. The second is a set of standards to interpret the information. In monitoring the plan, you need to know the following:

- Extent to which the desired actions were actually implemented.
- Effectiveness of those actions.

It is relatively easy to measure the extent to which actions were implemented. For example, has the accounting department installed the new accounting system? Has the production manager begun manufacturing the new product line? Is the outside consulting firm completing its market survey?

The *effectiveness* of actions is harder to determine. Many factors in the external environment over which the company has little if any control may be affecting the program. However, it can be valuable to attempt to isolate the marketing plan's effectiveness or outcomes, even if the effort is limited to only one or two major elements in the plan.

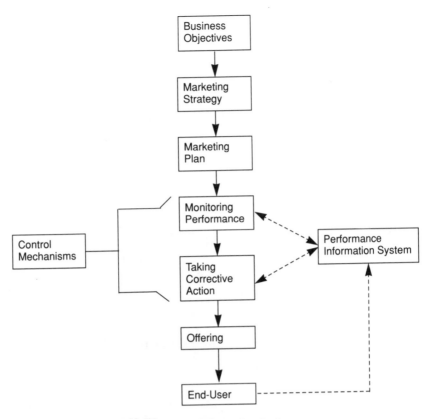

Figure 10.1　Control and Performance Information System

Source: David J. Luck and O.C. Farrell, *Marketing Strategy and Plans*, 2nd ed. (Englewood Cliffs, N.J.: Prentice–Hall, 1984):510. Copyright 1984. Adapted by permission of Prentice–Hall.

Control and Performance Information System

The marketing controller or product manager depends heavily on obtaining information. It would be difficult to describe all the kinds of data that this person might find valuable. We can only state that a regular and systematic flow of information is essential to control and monitoring, a flow that we label the control and performance information system. The place of this system in the total cycle of strategic planning is illustrated in Figure 10.1.

Notice that information flows both ways between the control and performance information system and the actual monitoring and correction stages. What is learned during monitoring performance or taking corrective action is fed back into the system. The information system is also influenced by feedback from end-users and affects the development of future marketing strategies.

The figure is somewhat simplified to give you the basic concept of how the system works. In reality, information does not come solely from end-users. It also comes from monitoring the flow of products through distribution channels and from data obtained on distributors, competitors, environmental changes, and internal activities of the firm itself. Some data are reported regularly through the accounting and marketing activities. Other data are gathered as needed and could include conducting market research to solve a product problem, defining particular market characteristics, or determining market position.

Control Standards and Criteria

It is impractical, if not impossible, to measure all the actions taken to implement a plan and measure all relevant environmental changes. You must select for your firm the key marketing and environmental variables that are to be measured and monitored.

Also, to establish control, you must set standards and criteria for evaluating results based on your marketing objectives. For example, what constitutes a deviation from budget? A 5 percent variance over or under planned figures? A 10 percent variance? How far does market share have to decline before it is considered a problem?

The chosen standards and criteria should reflect the uniqueness of your firm and its resources and should flow from the marketing

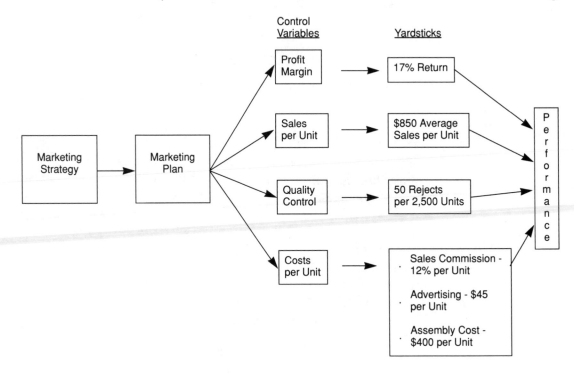

Figure 10.2   Variables Selected to Establish Yardsticks and to Control Performance

Source: David J. Luck and O.C. Farrell, *Marketing Strategy and Plans*, 2nd ed. (Englewood Cliffs, N.J.: Prentice–Hall, 1985):509. Copyright 1985. Adapted by permission of Prentice–Hall.

plan. Frequent comparison of the selected variables with the marketing plan yardsticks can help to keep the organization on course to reach its objectives.

An approach for setting key variables and standards/criteria for control is outlined briefly in Figure 10.2. Standards indicated in the figure are merely averages, but you can set various standards for categories of variables or establish a sliding scale.

Taking Corrective Action

Once a marketing controller or market planner has adequate comparisons of performance against standards, this person should determine whether any corrective action is needed. The first step in this process is *performance analysis*, in which the data are broken down to facilitate interpretation. This step is followed by *diagnosis* of the situation and its impact on the firm, and finally, by the *corrective action*, if any, that should be taken.

Performance Analysis

Performance analysis integrates the concepts of marketing strategy and plans with the concepts of managerial and cost accounting. As a result, it takes into consideration such planning variances as those found in sales, costs, and contribution margin, as shown in Figure 10.3.

This approach analyzes the differences between actual and planned performance. While it has limited potential for diagnosing the

Figure 10.3   Variance between Planned and Actual Performance, First Quarter (Single Product)

Item	Objective	Actual	Variance
Sales			
Units sold	435,000	432,000	(3,000)
Price per unit	$1.90	$2.11	+ $0.21
Dollar sales	$826,500	$911,520	+ $85,020
Total market (units)	22,000,000	26,000,000	+ 4,000,000
Share of market	1.9%	1.6%	(0.3)
Costs			
Variable cost per unit	$1.42	$1.56	+ $0.14
Total variable cost	$617,700	$673,920	
Contribution margin			
Per unit	$0.48	$0.55	+ $0.07
Total contribution	$208,800	$237,600	+ $28,800

Source: Format based on James M. Hulbert and Norman E. Toy, "Strategic Framework for Marketing Control," *Journal of Marketing* (April 1977):13. (Data are hypothetical.)

causes of problems, its major benefit lies in identifying areas where problems exist.

Diagnosis

In diagnosis, individual product managers examine the analyzed data and seek to explain a given problem and to determine its causes. Is the cause due to a sudden decline in consumer demand? Is it due to a rise in the cost of raw materials? Has a merger between two competitors blocked your firm from certain segments of the market? Is a promotional campaign having more or less impact than anticipated?

Once the cause or causes of a problem have been diagnosed, you need to assess their significance carefully. Does the firm need to take any action or will the problem solve itself given time? How much of an impact will it have on operations, profitability, earnings, advertising, and so on? Careful diagnosis of a problem can help you decide not only what action may be appropriate but whether any action needs to be taken at all.

Corrective Action

Corrective action to solve the problems you have diagnosed may range from minor adjustments to the plan to a major overhaul of assumptions and strategies, which requires falling back on contingency plans. Contingency planning, developed in the early stages of the market planning process, can be invaluable in the control and monitoring stages.

For example, if a sudden drop in consumer demand is the cause of declining sales, you may want to adopt a contingency plan of lowering prices and increasing promotion as a corrective action. Or you may want to phase out the product and reexamine your major strategic plan for the product line.

Use these guidelines when evaluating corrective actions:

- Can the factors that caused the problem be controlled by the firm?
- If so, what action would be effective?
- Is the action worth taking, based on the time, cost, and risks involved?
- If the factors cannot be controlled, how can the firm adjust to the situation?

Control and Future Market Planning

The information gained in the control and monitoring process brings us full circle to the beginning of a new strategic market planning cycle.

At the end of the current cycle, the company will have learned a great deal about the soundness of its strategies and objectives, the external and internal environment in which it operates, how well it adapts to unexpected problems or changes, and where it needs to be in the future to maintain or increase market share. This information can be used as the starting point for developing the next strategic marketing plan.

Well-planned and -executed control and monitoring activities can also increase the knowledge and planning skills of the firm's strategists. They will be more experienced in using the plan and in responding to deviations from strategic goals and tactical action plans. The more active and imaginative the control measures, the more the firm's strategists will learn.

Form 10: Control and Monitoring is designed to help you establish goals, standards or criteria, and tracking devices for your control and monitoring system. You should fill out a form for each of the key strategic objectives in your marketing plan.

Form 11: Budget Deviation Analysis can be used for monthly, quarterly, or yearly analysis to determine whether your budget is deviating from the plan. These two forms will help you to establish a proactive control system to evaluate how well the company is meeting its marketing objectives.

Summary

- Many companies tend to limit their control and monitoring efforts to tracking financial reports. You should have control yardsticks for every strategic objective in your plan, a standard or criterion for evaluating progress toward that objective, and tracking devices to monitor progress and help you to determine the causes of any deviations.

- Control can be defined as the action steps taken to keep the firm directed toward its objectives and to bring performance and desired results closer together. Control activities involve monitoring departmental and individual actions and taking steps either to match performance with desired results or to adjust objectives to match attainable performance levels.

- Some companies are establishing a marketing controller position. This individual monitors marketing expenses and activities and informs management about any deviations from plan.

- An effective control system enables the marketing controller or planner to detect when and where deviations from plan are occurring, determine the cause, and suggest corrective action.

- To achieve these aims, the controller or planner needs yardsticks and comparative standards, a feedback or performance information system, diagnostic ability and analytic system, and contingency plans and methods.

- A monitoring system can help a company know the extent to which the desired actions were actually implemented and how effective those actions were. The monitoring system has two main parts: a control and performance information system and a set of standards to interpret the information received.

- Corrective action follows these steps: (1) performance analysis to determine the difference between actual and planned performance, (2) diagnosis of any problems and their impact on the firm, and (3) action steps to correct problems.

- Information gained in the control and monitoring process is used as a starting point for the next strategic market planning cycle. Well-planned and -executed control and monitoring activities can increase the knowledge and planning skills of the firm's strategists.

Sample Case   "The Best Laid Plans . . ."

While the marketing team worked with department heads and managers on their implementation steps, Haines formed a special three-member task force to develop a monitoring and control system. He discovered in his research on DataStar that the company had no formal system for checking on progress toward goals or for detecting deviation from planned strategies.

Haines outlined what an effective control system would enable the task force to do.

"It should allow you to detect when and where deviations from planned results are occurring. For instance, if the sales force is making fewer sales after the telemarketing system is implemented, we need to take a look at what may be going wrong.

"Second, the system should enable you to determine the cause of the deviations from plan. Maybe communication lines between clerical staff and the sales force have broken down.

"Third, you should be able to suggest ways to correct the situation and to bring activities back in line with the plan. If the problem involves more than one department—say, operations and finance— we may need to create an interdepartmental task force to handle the situation."

Haines explained to the task force that they would develop yardsticks, standards, and tracking devices to monitor progress on marketing objectives and strategies. The task force would work closely with department heads and product managers to establish these elements, creating a regular and systematic flow of information from the various departments to the control and monitoring task force. If the task force detected any deviation from plan, they would then alert the appropriate department or manager and determine the cause and corrective action.

These procedures would build an ongoing performance information system for the company that could be used to monitor all future marketing plans. The task force could ensure that yardsticks other than purely financial information would be used to monitor and control the company's progress.

Form 10 shows the yardsticks, control standards, and tracking devices developed by the task force and product manager for AutoDrive. Haines wanted the group to monitor this product carefully, since Auto-Drive was to be launched nationwide.

DataStar introduced its hard disk drive amid a flurry of national advertising and promotional campaigns. By that time the new tele-marketing system was in place, and the company fully expected to realize their marketing objective of 12 percent market share per year.

The first three quarterly reports confirmed the most optimistic sales projections; the target consumer group was adopting the new product quickly, and the projected 12 percent sales figure was easily within reach. Early in the fourth quarter, however, the monitoring task force noticed a small but significant drop in sales.

They checked with a few of DataStar's customers who had yet to buy AutoDrive and discovered that one of their major competitors was about to enter the market with a hard disk drive of its own. The product was comparable to AutoDrive but would be priced $200 lower.

The development was a rude shock; market research had shown that this competitor would not be able to launch a comparable product until the second year of DataStar's marketing campaign. By that time, DataStar would have achieved at least a 20 percent share of the market.

Over the next few weeks, as the competitor's product penetrated the market, DataStar management watched their market share slowly but steadily erode in the final quarter. The competing hard disk drive was similar enough to DataStar's offering that many customers could not see the value of paying a higher price. Unless something was done quickly, DataStar would fall far short of its projected 12 percent market share by the end of the year.

The task force recommended abandoning the original high-price, high-promotion strategy and adopting a lower price, high-promotion approach. Management agreed and reduced AutoDrive's price by $100 and shifted to the contingency strategy of product differentiation. They emphasized AutoDrive's quality features and superior engineering, made certain add-on features standard items, designed a few changes in the product's appearance, and underscored DataStar's strong customer service and support.

The new marketing campaign was designed to convince consumers that DataStar's slightly higher price included far more value than the competition could offer. The lower price also meant DataStar could broaden its target markets and go after a wider range of customers.

The new strategy was clearly reflected in the budget, pushing up operating and G and A expenses. DataStar had to conduct additional market research, launch a new advertising campaign, broaden its telemarketing effort to reach the larger market, and seek out additional distribution channels to reach new customer segments. The deviation from planned budget figures is shown in the Budget Deviation Analysis that follows.

DataStar's control and monitoring system and its proactive strategic marketing plan enabled the company to detect and respond quickly to a sudden change in the external environment. Greg Haines and his marketing team had devised an alternative strategy that took advantage of the company's reputation for quality and its high level of consumer acceptance to stop the decline in market share.

Form 10 Control and Monitoring

Product: __AutoDrive__   Date: _____

1. Goal (yardstick derived from marketing objectives):

(1) Achieve 12 percent market share by end of first year.

(2) Realize ROI of 17 percent by end of first year.

(3) Migrate 22 percent of customers from old product to AutoDrive.

(4) Change collection from 2/10/30 to 2/15/45 to encourage dealers to carry larger stock.

2. Control standards or criteria:

(1) Quarterly sales and market share data.

(2) Return on investment.

---

(3) Current versus new customer list to check migration of customers from old to new

product.

(4) Sales to end-user versus quantity of product produced and shipped.

3. Tracking device:

(1) Actual sales results and market research.

(2) Net income before interest and taxes by product.

(3) Sales and customer listing data.

(4) Production runs of product.

Form 11 Budget Deviation Analysis

Product: __AutoDrive__   Date: _____

Profit or Loss as of 12/31/91

	Actual (A)	Budget (B)	Deviation (B – A)
Sales	$6,325,000	$7,905,000	$1,580,000
Cost of goods sold	3,795,000	4,743,000	948,000
Gross Margin	$2,530,000	$3,162,000	$ 632,000
Operating Expenses			
Advertising	$ 845,000	$ 633,000	$ (212,000)
Distribution	525,000	474,000	(51,000)
Market research	165,000	125,000	(40,000)
Salary	175,000	210,000	35,000
Miscellaneous	15,000	30,000	15,000
Total Operating Expenses	$1,725,000	$1,472,000	$ (253,000)
General/Administrative Expenses			
Salaries	$ 97,500	$ 74,250	$ (23,250)
Rent	17,250	14,500	(2,750)
Insurance	1,600	1,800	200
Supplies	4,300	5,600	1,300
Depreciation	16,250	13,850	(2,400)
Total G and A Expenses	$ 136,900	$ 110,000	$ (26,900)
Total Expenses	$1,861,900	$1,582,000	$ (279,900)
Net Profit (Loss) before Interest and Taxes	$ 668,100	$1,580,000	$ 911,900

Appendix

Instructions

A sound mission statement can help you to clarify your own thinking about the business your company is in and your overall goals. The statement should be brief yet present a clear and accurate definition of your business. Once you have written the mission statement, review it to determine whether it is

1. **Too narrow or too broad.** You don't want to limit your firm's mission, but neither do

you want to overestimate your reach.

2. **Realistic.** Is the mission compatible with your firm's potential for growth, its size, capacity, resources, employee skills, management expertise, and other factors?

3. **Profitable for stockholders.** Have you included the stockholders in the company mission?

Date: _____

Our Company's Mission Statement

_____

_____

_____

_____

_____

_____

_____

_____

_____

_____

_____

_____

_____

_____

_____

_____

_____

_____

Instructions

This questionnaire is designed to survey your current knowledge of the company's internal and external environment and of your key competitors. The purpose is to discover how much information is available and where the voids are in your data.

Fill out a questionnaire for each product your company markets. Have department heads and other appropriate staff members review the form and make comments. The broader your data base, the more you are likely to learn.

The following instructions should help you complete the questionnaire.

1. Identify the market segment in which you do business and enter it at the top of the form. If you compete in more than one defined segment or market, fill out separate forms for each product in that segment or market.

2. **Section A: Your firm's product offering.**

List the product you offer in a particular segment. If you offer more than one product in a segment or market, fill out a separate form for each product. (These forms will be correlated later to identify overlapping and to develop pricing structures.)

3. **Section B: Competitor products.**

After your product, list across the top the competitor's products that most directly compete with yours.

It may be that a competitor's products cannot be associated with any of yours in the same segment. You may want to list the closest competing product and assess it anyway, since that will give you a sense of the competitor's market coverage.

On the other hand, you may know of a competitor's product that competes with yours but be unable to assess it in any detail or with any degree of confidence. This fact would point out a void in your research. In that case, simply list the competing product and note that you could not assess it at this time.

4. **Section C: Quantitative or qualitative judgments.** Answer these questions about competitors *in the context of your respective situations.* For example, in question C–15., if your product is highly regulated in that segment, you would rate your own regulatory climate as "high."

In contrast, if your competitor's product is relatively free from regulation, you would rate the competitor's regulatory climate as "low." Compared with your company, the competitor enjoys a climate fairly free from restrictive regulation.

5. **Section D: Competitor information.**

Answer the questions in this section from the *competitor's viewpoint,* unless the question specifically asks you to compare the competitor's offering with your product.

Answer as many of the questions as you can. Where possible, research the questions you cannot answer. Remember, the questionnaire is not a test of anyone's ability but a survey of your current knowledge of the company's internal and external environment.

Competitor Names: _____   Date: _____

_____   Market/Product Manager: _____

_____

SECTION A: Our Product					
SECTION B: Competitor's Products					

SECTION C

1. Effectiveness of distribution channels (High–Medium–Low)					
2. Product life cycle stage (I-G-M-D)					
3. Product differentiation from competitors' offerings (H–M–L)					
4. Cyclicality of market segment (i.e., constant, seasonal) (H–M–L)					
5. Skills of the firms (all aspects) (H–M–L)					
6. Product quality/service levels perceived by customers (H–M–L)					
7. Flexibility of pricing structure (H–M–L)					
8. Price competitiveness (H–M–L)					
9. Substitution threat from competitors (H–M–L)					
10. Barriers to entry (H–M–L)					
11. Barriers to exit (H–M–L)					
12. Variety of applications and features (H–M–L)					
13. Capability for economies of scale (H–M–L)					
14. Raw materials easy to obtain (H–M–L)					
15. Regulatory climate (H–M–L)					
16. Risk in market segment (H–M–L)					
17. Required investment to stay competitive (H–M–L)					

18. Growth rate of total market (%)

19. Growth rate of product's market share (%)

20. Product's market share of total market (%)

21. Estimated profit margin (%)

22. Supplier power   (H–M–L)

23. Buyer power   (H–M–L)

NA = Not available or unknown.

SECTION D   Product: _____

Competitor: _____

1. Does this firm offer complementary products?

Their offering   Our product equivalent

_____   _____

_____   _____

_____   _____

_____   _____

2. Do they have technological advantages over our products?

Their offering and its advantages   Our product equivalent

_____   _____

_____   _____

_____   _____

_____   _____

3. Do they add value to any products above ours?

Their offering and its value added   Our product equivalent

_____   _____

_____   _____

_____   _____

4. Are they a niche company?

List niches and product offering in each   Our product equivalent

_____   _____

_____   _____

_____   _____

5. Is their pricing strategy by individual product, segment, or both?

List their pricing strategy

_____

_____

_____

6. What percent have they gone above or below the price of their product to make a sale?

Product offering and price variance   Our product equivalent

_____   _____

_____   _____

_____   _____

_____   _____

7. Do you feel this firm is cutting prices to gain market share for the long run? If yes, which products and how?

Product	Method of price cutting
_____	_____
_____	_____
_____	_____

8. What customer voids do their products fill that our product(s) do not?

Competitor's products	Associated customer voids
_____	_____
_____	_____
_____	_____
_____	_____

9. What type of distribution channels do they use?

_____

_____

_____

_____

10. What is the geographic coverage of their distribution system?

_____

_____

_____

_____

_____

11. What geographic area are they targeting as their market?

_____

_____

12. Do you feel this is an innovative firm?

_____

_____

_____

13. Is this firm a leader or follower?

_____

_____

14. Do customers see this firm's products as technologically superior or inferior to yours?

_____

_____

15. What product applications does this firm have above or below our offerings?

_____

_____

_____

16. List specific target markets/segments for each competitor product.

        Product   Target market/segment

_____   _____

_____   _____

_____   _____

_____   _____

Instructions

The Product Evaluation Questionnaire is designed to help you determine your products' current and projected positions based on the company's present strategies. Once you have completed your product evaluations, the results will guide you in formulating strategies to reposition your products to their desired projected positions.

Because conditions for each company differ, you may need to adapt the Product Evaluation Questionnaire for your firm. Follow these steps.

1. Go through the questionnaire and decide which questions you want to use. Add or delete questions to make the questionnaire more relevant to your company.

2. Decide which questions are *critical* to your product's success, which are of *medium* importance, and which are of *low* importance. Mark the questions with a C, M, or L under the Critical Success Ranking column.

3. Assign a point spread to each question based on whether it is critical, medium, or low in importance. We suggest the following scale:

Critical 1–10

Medium 1–7

Low 1–4

One is least important; 10, 7, 4 are most important. As a C, M, or L rank is assigned to each question, fill in the appropriate range of values in the Points Assigned column on the questionnaire.

4. Fill out your adjusted Product Evaluation Questionnaire and total the values for each of the three sections: Competitive Position, Market Attractiveness, and Business Strengths. These totals will be used as plot points to map your products on the matrices provided at the end of the questionnaire.

5. To determine the point values along the *horizontal* and *vertical* axes on the Business

Assessment Matrix and along the *vertical* axis on the Business Profile Matrix (the life cycle stage can be provided by the product manager), follow these steps.

(1) Add up the highest values assigned to the questions in the Points Assigned column for each section of the questionnaire.

(2) Divide these totals by the number of cells along the vertical axis in each matrix and the horizontal axis in the Business Assessment Matrix to obtain the point values for each axis. This will give you the incremental point values for each cell along each axis.

If the totals of the highest points are not equal for the vertical axes on both matrices, you may want to index the totals to 100. Indexing will not affect positioning of the products.

6. Add the total points under the current year and projected year columns for each section. These totals will give you the plotting points for the current and projected positions of each product on the matrices.

7. Plot your products' positions on the two matrices and write down any conclusions you may draw regarding product positions and adjustments to current strategies that may need to be made.

8. Fill out a Product Evaluation Questionnaire, Business Profile Matrix, and Business Assessment Matrix for each of your company's products.

The results of this questionnaire, although not 100 percent precise, will give you a starting point from which to quantify the data you have developed. This is particularly true for those items where little or no quantitative information is available.

The data you generate in filling out the questionnaire will be used to complete the Business Profile and Business Assessment matrices, along with Form 4 Growth-Share Matrix.

Product: _____   Date: _____

I. Competitive Postition   Critical Success Factors Ranking (C, M, L)

Points Assigned: Critical _____   Medium _____   Low _____

1. __ Price
   To what extent does our firm have price advantage over major competitors?

	Current	Projected	Points Assigned
Low	_____	_____	_____
Moderate	_____	_____	_____
High	_____	_____	_____

Comments

_____

_____

2. __ Quality
   To what extent does our firm have better product quality than our major competitors?

	Current	Projected	Points Assigned
Low	_____	_____	_____
Same	_____	_____	_____
Somewhat higher	_____	_____	_____
Much higher	_____	_____	_____

Comments

_____

_____

_____

3. __ Percent of market

	Current	Projected	Points Assigned
Low			
Medium			
High			

Comments

_____

_____

4. __ Variety
   To what extent does our firm have a broader assortment associated with this product than do our major competitors?

	Current	Projected	Points Assigned
Less			
Equal			
Moderate			
High			

Comments

_____

_____

5. __ Sales personnel
   How does our firm's sales staff compare with our major competitors'?

	Current	Projected	Points Assigned
Low			
Equal			
Better			

Comments

_____

_____

6. __ Breadth of product application

	Current	Projected	Points Assigned
Narrow	_____	_____	_____
Average	_____	_____	_____
Broad	_____	_____	_____

Comments

_____

_____

_____

7. __ Relation to other product lines

	Current	Projected	Points Assigned
Little/no compatibility	_____	_____	_____
Moderate	_____	_____	_____
Good	_____	_____	_____
Excellent	_____	_____	_____

Comments

_____

_____

_____

8. __ Service
   How does our firm's service compare with major competitors'?

	Current	Projected	Points Assigned
Less	_____	_____	_____
Same	_____	_____	_____
Moderately better	_____	_____	_____
High	_____	_____	_____

Comments

_____

_____

9. __ Growth of competition

	Current	Projected	Points Assigned
Low	_____	_____	_____
Moderate	_____	_____	_____
High	_____	_____	_____

Comments

_____

_____

10. __ Assortment
    To what extent does our firm have broader assortment than our major competitor has?

	Current	Projected	Points Assigned
Low	_____	_____	_____
Same	_____	_____	_____
Moderately higher	_____	_____	_____
High	_____	_____	_____

Comments

_____

_____

11. __ Supplier power
    To what extent can suppliers exert pressure over necessary resources and possibly enter our market?

	Current	Projected	Points Assigned
Low	_____	_____	_____
Medium	_____	_____	_____
High	_____	_____	_____

Comments

_____

_____

12. __ Substitution threat
    To what extent can competitors produce and supply equal or better substitute products over our offering?

	Current	Projected	Points Assigned
Low	_____	_____	_____
Medium	_____	_____	_____
High	_____	_____	_____

Comments

_____

_____

_____

Total Points—Competitive Position: _____ _____

Competitive Position—High Points Total: _____

II. Market Attractiveness   Critical Success Factors Ranking (C, M, L)

Points Assigned: Critical _____   Medium _____   Low _____

1. __ Required investment

	Current	Projected	Points Assigned
Low			
Medium			
High			

2. __ New competitive threat

	Current	Projected	Points Assigned
Low			
Moderate			
High			

Comments

3. __ Risk
New products, new competitors, new fashions

	Current	Projected	Points Assigned
Low			
Moderate			
High			

Comments

_____

_____

_____

4. __ Product life expectancy

	Current	Projected	Points Assigned
Low	_____	_____	_____
Moderate	_____	_____	_____
High	_____	_____	_____

Comments

_____

_____

_____

5. __ Price elasticity to market demand

	Current	Projected	Points Assigned
Demand greatly reduced as price rises	_____	_____	_____
Demand moderately reduced	_____	_____	_____
Demand slightly reduced	_____	_____	_____
Demand not affected	_____	_____	_____

Comments

_____

_____

_____

_____

6. ___ Market growth—dollars

	Current	Projected	Points Assigned
Declining			
Stationary			
Moderate			
Good			

Comments

_____

_____

_____

7. ___ Cyclicality (of demand)

	Current	Projected	Points Assigned
Fluctuating			
Moderate			
Stable			

Comments

_____

_____

8. ___ Market size—$ volume (000)

	Current	Projected	Points Assigned
To $300			
$301 to $600			
$601 to $1,000			
More than $1,000			

Comments

_____

_____

9. __ Profitability—actual or estimated

	Current	Projected	Points Assigned
Red	_____	_____	_____
0–5%	_____	_____	_____
6–11%	_____	_____	_____
12% and above	_____	_____	_____

Comments

_____

_____

10. __ Segmentation
How easily can the market for this product be segmented?

	Current	Projected	Points Assigned
Difficult	_____	_____	_____
Moderately easy	_____	_____	_____
Easy	_____	_____	_____

Comments

_____

_____

11. __ Seasonality

	Current	Projected	Points Assigned
Yes	_____	_____	_____
Partial	_____	_____	_____
None	_____	_____	_____

Comments

_____

_____

12. __ Regulatory climate
How much are quality, specifications, price, environmental concerns affected?

	Current	Projected	Points Assigned
Little or none	_____	_____	_____
Moderately regulated	_____	_____	_____
Highly regulated	_____	_____	_____

Comments

_____

_____

13. __ Customer negotiating/buyer power

	Current	Projected	Points Assigned
Low	_____	_____	_____
Moderate	_____	_____	_____
High	_____	_____	_____

Comments

_____

_____

14. __ Return on investment (compared to company yardstick)

	Current	Projected	Points Assigned
Low	_____	_____	_____
Moderate	_____	_____	_____
High	_____	_____	_____

Comments

_____

_____

_____

15. ___ Distribution

	Current	Projected	Points Assigned
Poor	_____	_____	_____
Average	_____	_____	_____
Good	_____	_____	_____
Excellent	_____	_____	_____

Comments

_____

_____

_____

16. ___ Lateral effect on sales of companion products

	Current	Projected	Points Assigned
Low	_____	_____	_____
Medium	_____	_____	_____
High	_____	_____	_____

Comments

_____

_____

_____

_____

17. __ Transactions generated

	Current	Projected	Points Assigned
1 purchase every 3 years or longer	_____	_____	_____
1 purchase every 2 to 3 years or longer	_____	_____	_____
1 purchase every 1 to 2 years	_____	_____	_____
1 purchase every 6 months to 1 year	_____	_____	_____

Comments

_____

_____

_____

Total Points—Market Attractiveness: _____ _____

Market Attractiveness—High Points Total: _____

III. Business Strengths   Critical Success Factors Ranking (C, M, L)

Points Assigned: Critical _____ Medium _____ Low _____

1. __ Geographic coverage

	Current	Projected	Points Assigned
Limited	_____	_____	_____
Moderate	_____	_____	_____
Large	_____	_____	_____

Comments

_____

_____

_____

2. __ Distribution (current system)

	Current	Projected	Points Assigned
Poor			
Average			
Good			
Excellent			

Comments

_____

_____

3. __ Product servicing
   How does our firm's repair/servicing compare with that of competitors?

	Current	Projected	Points Assigned
Low			
Equal			
Better			

Comments

_____

_____

4. __ Change in market share—three-year historical trend. If less than three years, use available data.

	Current	Projected	Points Assigned
Declining			
Stationary			
Moderately increasing			
Greatly increasing			

Comments

_____

_____

5. __ Selling power

	Current	Projected	Points Assigned
Low	_____	_____	_____
Below average	_____	_____	_____
Average	_____	_____	_____
High	_____	_____	_____

Comments

_____

_____

6. __ Price competitiveness

	Current	Projected	Points Assigned
Low	_____	_____	_____
Moderate	_____	_____	_____
High	_____	_____	_____

Comments

_____

_____

7. __ Breadth of product line

	Current	Projected	Points Assigned
Narrow	_____	_____	_____
Average	_____	_____	_____
Broad	_____	_____	_____

Comments

_____

_____

_____

8. __ New products
   To what extent do new products or variations of present products enter our business
   and stimulate customers to purchase?

	Current	Projected	Points Assigned
Seldom	_____	_____	_____
Occasionally	_____	_____	_____
Average	_____	_____	_____

Comments

_____

_____

_____

9. __ Product differentiation

	Current	Projected	Points Assigned
Difficult	_____	_____	_____
Moderately difficult	_____	_____	_____
Easy	_____	_____	_____

Comments

_____

_____

_____

_____

10. ___ Market share

	Current	Projected	Points Assigned
0–7%			
8–14%			
15–21%			
22–30%			
31% and over			

Comments

_____

_____

11. ___ Source structure

	Current	Projected	Points Assigned
Poor			
Fair			
Average			
Good			

Comments

_____

_____

12. ___ Product quality
    To what extent does our firm have better quality than our competitors?

	Current	Projected	Points Assigned
Lower			
Same			
Moderately higher			
Higher			

Comments

_____

_____

13. ___ Compatibility

    A. To what extent do our systems satisfy needs of our product line?

	Current	Projected	Points Assigned
Little or no compatibility	_____	_____	_____
Moderate	_____	_____	_____
Good	_____	_____	_____
Excellent	_____	_____	_____

Comments

_____

_____

_____

    ___ B. Relation to other lines within our product group

	Current	Projected	Points Assigned
Little or no compatibility	_____	_____	_____
Moderate	_____	_____	_____
Good	_____	_____	_____

Comments

_____

_____

_____

_____

__ C. Corporate strategy and other product lines

	Current	Projected	Points Assigned
Little or no compatibility	_____	_____	_____
Moderate	_____	_____	_____
Good	_____	_____	_____
Excellent	_____	_____	_____

Comments

_____

_____

_____

14. __ Drawing power

	Current	Projected	Points Assigned
Poor	_____	_____	_____
Below average	_____	_____	_____
Average	_____	_____	_____
High	_____	_____	_____

Comments

_____

_____

_____

_____

Total Points—Business Strengths: _____   _____

Business Strengths—High Points Total: _____

Product: _____   Date: _____

Total Points—Competitive Position: 19__ ____
                                           19__ ____

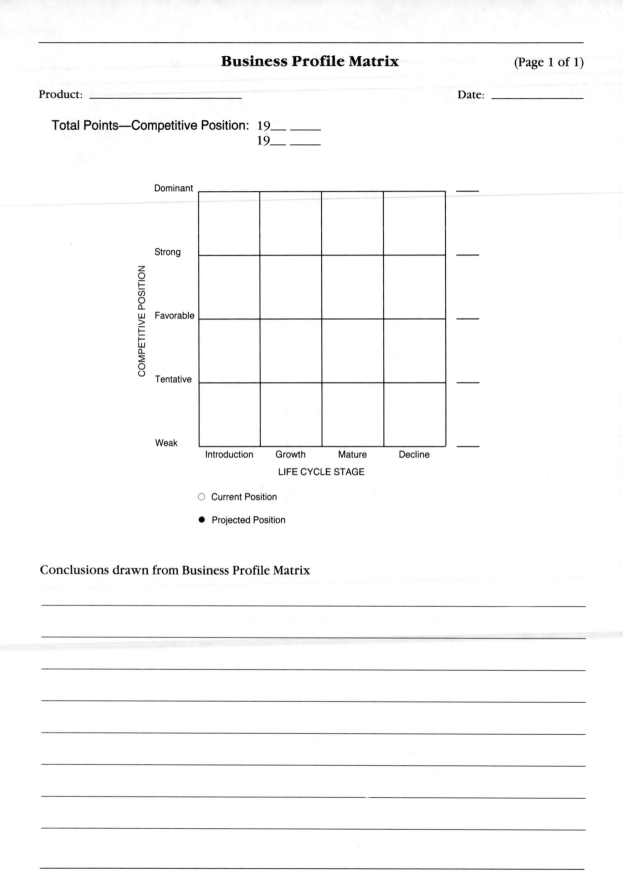

○ Current Position

● Projected Position

Conclusions drawn from Business Profile Matrix

_____

_____

_____

_____

_____

_____

_____

_____

Business Assessment Matrix

Product: _____   Date: _____

Total Points—Market Attractiveness: 19__ ____   19__ ____
Total Points—Business Strengths: 19__ ____   19__ ____

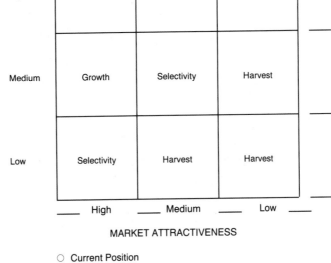

Conclusions drawn from Business Assessment Matrix.

_____

_____

_____

_____

_____

_____

_____

_____

_____

Form 4 Modified Growth–Share Matrix

Instructions

The Growth–Share Matrix enables you to see the current and projected positions of your product lines in a macro or portfolio view, based on your current strategies. You can then decide whether you need to change your strategies to improve the performance of your products in the future.

To complete the matrix, follow these steps:

1. Establish values for the market share and growth rate dividing lines; these values are strategically important since they serve as cutoff points in your assessment of your portfolio. You can use either percentages or a log scale for the horizontal axis.

2. Using the information obtained from the Product Evaluation Questionnaire, plot the current and projected positions of all product lines on the matrix.

Write down any conclusions drawn from the Modified Growth–Share Matrix regarding product repositioning and adjustments to current strategies that may be needed.

The information shown on the Modified Growth–Share Matrix can help you to determine which products are following a success sequence and which products may need to be repositioned or eliminated from your portfolio.

Product: _____   Date: _____

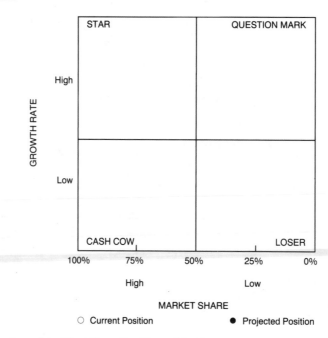

Conclusions drawn from Modified Growth–Share Matrix

_____

_____

_____

_____

Form 5   Problem Analysis

Instructions

The Problem Analysis form will help you to identify and analyze problems facing your firm now and in the near future. Make sure you include all problems regardless of size; often it's the small ones that can do the most harm in the long run.

After listing the problems, fill out the rest of the form in the following steps:

1. Rank the problems according to their importance to your firm.

2. Determine whether the problems are industry or company problems.

3. Examine the problems and determine whether two or more share a single cause.

4. Separate the problems into those that can be solved and those that for various reasons cannot be solved.

5. List action steps that can be taken to deal with those problems over which you have some control.

6. Determine which problems may represent opportunities.

The purpose of this analysis is to get beyond symptoms to the core problems. The core problems, if solvable, are the ones you want to list in your marketing plan, along with your proposed action steps to address them.

Product: _____   Date: _____

Problems

1. List all problems:

_____

_____

_____

_____

_____

2. a. Rank problems in order of their importance to your firm:

_____

_____

_____

_____

_____

_____

b. List problems that share a single cause:

Problems	Cause
_____	_____
_____	_____
_____	_____
_____	_____
_____	_____

3. a. Industry-related problems:

_____

_____

_____

b. Company-related problems

_____

_____

_____

4. a. Problems that can be solved (over which you have some control):

_____

_____

_____

b. Problems that cannot be solved (over which you have little or no control):

_____

_____

_____

_____

5. Action steps that can be taken to solve problems:

Problem

Action Steps

_____   _____

_____   _____

_____   _____

_____   _____

_____   _____

_____   _____

_____   _____

_____   _____

6. Problems that can be turned into opportunities:

Problem

Possible Opportunity

_____   _____

_____   _____

_____   _____

_____   _____

_____   _____

_____   _____

_____   _____

_____   _____

_____   _____

Instructions

This form will help you to identify and take advantage of opportunities available to your firm. Your first step is to list all opportunities, no matter how improbable they may seem, in particular considering any opportunities associated with the following:

Specific company strengths
Changing consumer lifestyles
Market coverage
Distribution structure
Organization structure
Geographic coverage
Improvements in production or service
  facilities
Product advantages
New technologies
Financial/resource advantages
Changing customer wants
New applications of existing products

Once you have listed the opportunities, fill out the remainder of the form in the following steps:

1. Rank the opportunities in order of their importance or contribution value to your firm.

2. Determine which opportunities are most compatible with your company.

3. Assign numeric values (e.g., 1–10) to the opportunities you have selected. Use a scale of 0%–100% for the horizontal axis, Probability of Success, on the Opportunity Matrix.

4. Plot these opportunities on the Opportunity Matrix.

5. Develop action steps to realize the strongest potential opportunities.

6. Identify the resources available to develop the opportunities.

Product: _____   Date: _____

Opportunities

1. List all potential opportunities

_____

_____

_____

_____

2. Determine which opportunities are most compatible with your firm:

_____

_____

_____

_____

_____

3. Assess opportunities in terms of attractiveness to firm and probability of success:

Opportunity	Attractiveness to firm*	Probability of success
_____	_____	_____
_____	_____	_____
_____	_____	_____

*Scale is from 1 to 10, with 10 indicating greatest attractiveness to the firm.

4. Plot opportunities on Opportunity Matrix.

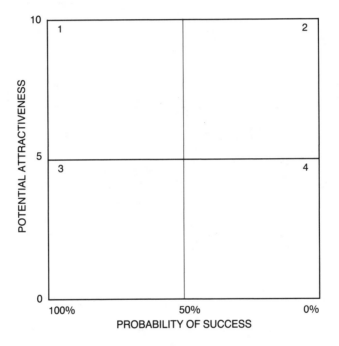

5. List opportunities selected and action steps developed to realize them:

Opportunities	Action Steps
_____	_____
_____	_____
_____	_____
_____	_____

Resources

1. Financial resources available to develop opportunities:

    Opportunities   Financial Resources

    _____   _____

    _____   _____

    _____   _____

    _____   _____

2. Personnel needed to develop opportunities:

a. Management:

_____

_____

b. Research and Development:

_____

_____

c. Manufacturing:

_____

_____

d. Sales:

_____

_____

e. Marketing:

_____

_____

_____

3. Raw materials needed:

Raw Material	Difficult to source	Moderately difficult	Moderately easy	Easy to source
_____	_____	_____	_____	_____
_____	_____	_____	_____	_____
_____	_____	_____	_____	_____
_____	_____	_____	_____	_____

4. Advertising effort needed to develop opportunities:

Opportunities	Advertising Effort
_____	_____
_____	_____
_____	_____
_____	_____
_____	_____

5. Distribution channels needed:

Opportunities	Distribution Channels
_____	_____
_____	_____
_____	_____
_____	_____
_____	_____
_____	_____

Instructions

This form is designed to help you establish your strategic marketing objectives by marketing mix and other functional areas associated with your product lines. By clarifying your objectives, you will be able to develop strategies to achieve them.

To complete the form, follow these steps:

1. List overall company marketing objectives.

2. Fill out product marketing objectives for each element of the marketing mix and any other areas you feel are important.

When developing your objectives, make sure they are as follows:

Measurable—Use specific goals, dates, and percentages, etc. by which progress toward objectives can be measured.

Realistic—Base your objectives on a sound assessment of the company's resources and conditions.

Attainable—You can reasonably attain your objectives within the time frame stipulated.

Product: _____   Date: _____

I. Overall Marketing Objectives
List and describe overall marketing objectives:

_____

_____

_____

_____

_____

_____

_____

_____

_____

_____

_____

_____

_____

_____

_____

II. Product Marketing Objectives
List and describe marketing objectives for each major marketing criterion:

Profitability

Pricing

_____

_____

_____

_____

_____

_____

_____

_____

_____

Market Share

Promotion/Advertising

_____

_____

_____

_____

_____

_____

_____

_____

Distribution

Product Development

_____

_____

_____

_____

_____

_____

_____

Sales Volume

Other (training, customer relations, service)

_____

_____

_____

_____

_____

_____

_____

_____

Instructions

This Marketing Strategies form can help you to clarify your marketing strategies and to formulate contingency plans. To complete the form, follow these steps:

1. List the objectives for each element of the marketing mix.

2. Fill in selected strategies to achieve marketing objectives.

3. Briefly state contingency strategies for each element of the marketing mix.

Once you have selected your primary and contingency strategies, evaluate them in terms of internal compatibility with company objectives, external compatibility with market conditions, available resources within the company, time frames established in the objectives, and risk factors involved in achieving your objectives.

Product: _____   Date: _____

I. Product Objectives and Strategies

1. Describe product objectives:

_____

_____

_____

_____

2. Describe product strategies:

_____

_____

_____

3. Describe briefly contingency strategies and under what conditions they would be implemented:

_____

_____

_____

_____

_____

II. Pricing Objectives and Strategies

1. Describe pricing objectives for the product:

_____

_____

_____

_____

_____

_____

2. Describe pricing strategies for the product:

_____

_____

_____

_____

_____

_____

3. Describe briefly contingency strategies and under what conditions they would be
    implemented:

_____

_____

_____

_____

_____

_____

III. Promotion/Advertising Objectives and Strategies

1. Describe promotion/advertising objectives for product:

_____

_____

_____

_____

_____

_____

2. Describe promotion/advertising strategies for product:

_____

_____

_____

_____

_____

_____

3. Describe briefly contingency strategies and under what conditions they would be
    implemented:

_____

_____

_____

_____

_____

_____

IV. Distribution Objectives and Strategies

1. Describe distribution objectives for product:

_____

_____

_____

_____

_____

_____

2. Describe distribution strategies for product:

_____

_____

_____

_____

_____

_____

3. Describe briefly contingency strategies and under what conditions they would be
   implemented:

_____

_____

_____

_____

_____

_____

V. Other Objectives and Strategies
1. Describe other objectives for product:

_____

_____

_____

_____

_____

_____

2. Describe other strategies for product:

_____

_____

_____

_____

_____

_____

3. Describe briefly contingency strategies and under what conditions they would be
    implemented:

_____

_____

_____

_____

_____

_____

_____

Instructions

Implementation is one of the most important and overlooked steps in the planning process. This form is designed to help you develop a strategy for presenting and implementing your new marketing plan to ensure that it has the best chance for success.

To complete the form, follow these steps:

1. List the members of top management who must approve and endorse the new marketing plan.

2. Set up a schedule for presenting the new plan to top management, department heads, and other appropriate managers or staff members.

3. Identify all potential organizational and behavioral problems that may arise during implementation.

4. Develop suggested strategies for avoiding or handling these problems.

Keep the list of problems and strategies confidential. Handling conflicts is often a delicate matter in the best of circumstances; you do not want your implementation strategy to create problems.

Product: _____   Date: _____

1. Members of top management who must approve and endorse the new marketing plan:

_____

_____

_____

_____

_____

_____

2. Schedule of presentations:

Group	Date of presentation
_____	_____
_____	_____
_____	_____
_____	_____
_____	_____
_____	

3. Potential organizational and behavioral problems that may arise during implementation:

_____

_____

_____

_____

_____

_____

_____

_____

4. Suggested strategies for preventing or handling organizational and behavioral problems:

_____

_____

_____

_____

_____

_____

_____

_____

_____

_____

Instructions

The Control and Monitoring form will help you to establish your goals, standards or criteria, and tracking devices for your control and monitoring system. Fill out a form for each of the key strategic objectives in your marketing plan. The information generated by these forms can be fed into your Control and Performance Information System and help you to keep your company on track toward its objectives.

Complete the form by following these steps:

1. State the goal you wish to establish, based on your marketing objectives.

2. Describe the control standards or criteria you will use to judge progress toward achieving that goal.

3. Describe the tracking device that will be used to measure progress toward the goal; the tracking devices will act as an early warning system to detect problems.

Product: _____   Date: _____

1. Goal (yardstick derived from marketing objectives):_____

_____

_____

_____

_____

2. Control standards or criteria: _____

_____

_____

_____

_____

_____

3. Tracking device: _____

_____

_____

_____

_____

_____

Instructions

This form is designed to be used for monthly, quarterly, or yearly financial analysis to determine whether your budget is deviating from the plan. Together with Form 10 Control and Monitoring, these two forms can help you to establish a proactive control system to evaluate how well your company is meeting its marketing objectives.

To complete the form, follow these steps:

1. Fill in the proposed budget figures for all categories.

2. Fill in actual expenditures for each category.

3. Subtract the actual expenditures column (A) from the proposed budget column (B) to determine any deviation from the planned budget.

Product: _____   Date: _____

Profit or Loss as of 12/31/19—

	Actual (A)	Budget (B)	Deviation (B – A)
Sales	$	$	$
Cost of goods sold	_____	_____	_____
Gross Margin	$	$	$
Operating Expenses			
Advertising	$	$	$
Distribution			
Market research			
Salary			
Miscellaneous	_____	_____	_____
Total Operating Expenses	$	$	$
General/Administrative Expenses			
Salaries	$	$	$
Rent			
Insurance			
Supplies			
Depreciation	_____	_____	_____
Total G and A Expenses	$	$	$
Total Expenses	$	$	$
Net Profit (Loss) before Interest and Taxes	$	$	$

Index

About the Authors

ROBERT J. HAMPER has been with the former Bell System for ten years and has held a variety of departmental positions in such areas as market analysis, economic evaluation, market management, and financial management. At Bell, he designed and implemented practical applications of portfolio theory and optimization modeling of resource allocation to the strategic marketing process. His work included designing product planning systems for use by the marketing staff.

Mr. Hamper also has worked at AT&T and with Bell Laboratories on modeling techniques for practical use in financial and strategic market planning. These techniques have been adopted by other Bell System companies. He holds a bachelor of science degree and a master's degree in business administration from Illinois State University and is an adjunct assistant professor in the Graduate School of Business at Rosary College, River Forest, Illinois.

L. SUE BAUGH served as senior editor for six years at the management consultant firm Booz, Allen & Hamilton. She is currently an independent business writer and has contributed to and edited numerous books on marketing, finance, and related business topics for such publishers as Richard D. Irwin; Scott, Foresman and Company; Houghton Mifflin Company; and the Wm C Brown Group.

Ms. Baugh is the author of *Foodservice: A Segmented Industry,* an in-depth marketing survey of the foodservice industry developed for the International Foodservice Manufacturers Association, and *Handbook for Business Writing,* a reference and style guide for business communications. Ms. Baugh holds a bachelor's degree from the University of Iowa and a master's degree from the University of North Carolina.